Childcare Act 2006

CHAPTER 21

Explanatory Notes are available separately

GRAN*GIS* UK Publishing

Adapted and published by GRANGIS (Grand Register Library).
Online: www.grangis.com
E-mail: contact@grangis.com

In this version:
ISBN: 979-8-88559-076-1

Note: This is the original version (as it was originally enacted). Title, sub-title and the generated date is as marked on the page.

Childcare Act 2006

CHAPTER 21

CONTENTS

PART 1

GENERAL FUNCTIONS OF LOCAL AUTHORITY: ENGLAND

Improvement of young children's well-being

Provision of childcare

Information, advice and assistance

Miscellaneous

CHAPTER 4

VOLUNTARY REGISTRATION

CHAPTER 5

COMMON PROVISIONS

Childcare Act 2006

2006 CHAPTER 21

An Act to make provision about the powers and duties of local authorities and other bodies in England in relation to the improvement of the well-being of young children; to make provision about the powers and duties of local authorities in England and Wales in relation to the provision of childcare and the provision of information to parents and other persons; to make provision about the regulation and inspection of childcare provision in England; to amend Part 10A of the Children Act 1989 in relation to Wales; and for connected purposes. [11th July 2006]

BE IT ENACTED by the Queen's most Excellent Majesty, by and with the advice and consent of the Lords Spiritual and Temporal, and Commons, in this present Parliament assembled, and by the authority of the same, as follows:—

PART 1

GENERAL FUNCTIONS OF LOCAL AUTHORITY: ENGLAND

Improvement of young children's well-being

1 General duties of local authority in relation to well-being of young children

(1) An English local authority must—
   (a) improve the well-being of young children in their area, and
   (b) reduce inequalities between young children in their area in relation to the matters mentioned in subsection (2).

(2) In this Act "well-being", in relation to children, means their well-being so far as relating to—
   (a) physical and mental health and emotional well-being;
   (b) protection from harm and neglect;

(c) education, training and recreation;
(d) the contribution made by them to society;
(e) social and economic well-being.

(3) The Secretary of State may, in accordance with regulations, set targets for—
(a) the improvement of the well-being of young children in the area of an English local authority;
(b) the reduction of inequalities between young children in the area of an English local authority in relation to the matters mentioned in subsection (2).

(4) In exercising their functions, an English local authority must act in the manner that is best calculated to secure that any targets set under subsection (3) (so far as relating to the area of the local authority) are met.

(5) In performing their duties under this section, an English local authority must have regard to any guidance given from time to time by the Secretary of State.

2 Meaning of "early childhood services" for purposes of section 3

(1) In section 3 "early childhood services", in relation to an English local authority, means—
(a) early years provision;
(b) the social services functions of the local authority, so far as relating to young children, parents or prospective parents;
(c) health services relating to young children, parents or prospective parents;
(d) the provision, under arrangements made under section 2 of the Employment and Training Act 1973 (c. 50), of assistance to parents or prospective parents;
(e) the service provided by the local authority under section 12 (duty to provide information and assistance) so far as relating to parents or prospective parents.

(2) In this section—

"parent" means a parent of a young child, and includes any individual who—
(a) has parental responsibility for a young child, or
(b) has care of a young child;

"prospective parent" means a pregnant woman or any other person who is likely to become, or is planning to become, a parent;

"social services functions", in relation to a local authority, has the same meaning as in the Local Authority Social Services Act 1970 (c. 42).

3 Specific duties of local authority in relation to early childhood services

(1) For the purpose of their general duty under section 1(1), an English local authority have the further duties imposed by subsections (2) and (3).

(2) The authority must make arrangements to secure that early childhood services in their area are provided in an integrated manner which is calculated to—
(a) facilitate access to those services, and
(b) maximise the benefit of those services to parents, prospective parents and young children.

(3) The authority must take steps—

(a) to identify parents or prospective parents in the authority's area who would otherwise be unlikely to take advantage of early childhood services that may be of benefit to them and their young children, and

(b) to encourage those parents or prospective parents to take advantage of those services.

(4) An English local authority must take all reasonable steps to encourage and facilitate the involvement in the making and implementation of arrangements under this section of—

(a) parents and prospective parents in their area,

(b) early years providers in their area, including those in the private and voluntary sectors, and

(c) other persons engaged in activities which may improve the well-being of young children in their area.

(5) In discharging their duties under this section, an English local authority must have regard to such information about the views of young children as is available to the local authority and appears to them to be relevant to the discharge of those duties.

(6) In discharging their duties under this section, an English local authority must have regard to any guidance given from time to time by the Secretary of State.

(7) In this section—

"early years provider" has the same meaning as in Part 3;

"parent" and "prospective parent" have the same meaning as in section 2.

4 Duty of local authority and relevant partners to work together

(1) For the purposes of this section each of the following is a relevant partner of an English local authority—

(a) a Strategic Health Authority or Primary Care Trust for an area any part of which falls within the area of the local authority;3

(b) the Secretary of State, in relation to his functions under section 2 of the Employment and Training Act 1973 (c. 50).

(2) An English local authority must make arrangements to work with each of the authority's relevant partners in the performance by the authority of their duties under sections 1 and 3.

(3) Each of the relevant partners of an English local authority must work with the authority and with the other relevant partners in the making of the arrangements.

(4) An English local authority and each of their relevant partners may for the purposes of arrangements under this section—

(a) provide staff, goods, services, accommodation or other resources;

(b) establish and maintain a pooled fund.

(5) For the purposes of subsection (4) a pooled fund is a fund—

(a) which is made up of contributions by the authority and the relevant partner or partners concerned, and

(b) out of which payments may be made towards expenditure incurred in the discharge of functions of the authority and functions of the relevant partner or partners.

(6) An English local authority and each of their relevant partners falling within subsection (1)(a) must, in exercising their functions under this section, have regard to any guidance given from time to time by the Secretary of State.

5 Power to amend sections 2 and 4

The Secretary of State may by order—

(a) amend the definition of "early childhood services" in section 2(1), and

(b) in connection with any amendment of that definition, make such other amendments of section 2 or 4 as appear to him to be necessary or expedient.

Provision of childcare

6 Duty to secure sufficient childcare for working parents

(1) An English local authority must secure, so far as is reasonably practicable, that the provision of childcare (whether or not by them) is sufficient to meet the requirements of parents in their area who require childcare in order to enable them—

(a) to take up, or remain in, work, or

(b) to undertake education or training which could reasonably be expected to assist them to obtain work.

(2) In determining for the purposes of subsection (1) whether the provision of childcare is sufficient to meet those requirements, a local authority—

(a) must have regard to the needs of parents in their area for—

(i) the provision of childcare in respect of which the child care element of working tax credit is payable, and

(ii) the provision of childcare which is suitable for disabled children, and

(b) may have regard to any childcare which they expect to be available outside their area.

(3) In discharging their duty under subsection (1), a local authority must have regard to any guidance given from time to time by the Secretary of State.

(4) The Secretary of State may by order amend subsection (2) (and subsection (6) so far as relating to that subsection) so as to modify the matters to which a local authority must or may have regard in determining whether the provision of childcare is sufficient.

(5) Except in relation to a disabled child, this section does not apply in relation to childcare for a child on or after the 1st September next following the date on which he attains the age of 14.

(6) In this section—

"child care element", in relation to working tax credit, is to be read in accordance with section 12 of the Tax Credits Act 2002 (c. 21);

"disabled child" means a child who has a disability for the purposes of the Disability Discrimination Act 1995 (c. 50);

"parent" includes any individual who—

(a) has parental responsibility for a child, or

(b) has care of a child.

7 Duty to secure prescribed early years provision free of charge

(1) An English local authority must secure that early years provision of a prescribed description is available free of charge for such periods as may be prescribed for each young child in their area who—

(a) has attained such age as may be prescribed, but

(b) is under compulsory school age.

(2) In discharging their duty under subsection (1), a local authority must have regard to any guidance given from time to time by the Secretary of State.

8 Powers of local authority in relation to the provision of childcare

(1) An English local authority may—

(a) assist any person who provides or proposes to provide childcare;

(b) make arrangements with any other person for the provision of childcare;

(c) subject to subsection (3), provide childcare.

(2) The assistance which a local authority may give under subsection (1)(a) includes financial assistance; and the arrangements which a local authority may make under subsection (1)(b) include arrangements involving the provision of financial assistance by the authority.

(3) An English local authority may not provide childcare for a particular child or group of children unless the local authority are satisfied—

(a) that no other person is willing to provide the childcare (whether in pursuance of arrangements made with the authority or otherwise), or

(b) if another person is willing to do so, that in the circumstances it is appropriate for the local authority to provide the childcare.

(4) Subsection (3) does not affect the provision of childcare by the governing body of a maintained school.

(5) Subsection (3) does not apply in relation to the provision of childcare under section 18(1) or (5) of the Children Act 1989 (c. 41) (day care for children in need).

(6) In exercising their functions under this section, an English local authority must have regard to any guidance given from time to time by the Secretary of State.

9 Arrangements between local authority and childcare providers

(1) This section applies where an English local authority make arrangements with a person (other than the governing body of a maintained school) for the provision by that person of childcare in consideration of financial assistance provided by the authority under the arrangements.

(2) The local authority must exercise their functions with a view to securing that the provider of the childcare meets any requirements imposed on him by the arrangements.

(3) The requirements imposed by the arrangements may, in particular, if any specified conditions are not satisfied, require the repayment of the whole or any part of any financial assistance provided by the local authority under the arrangements.

10 Charges where local authority provide childcare

(1) An English local authority may enter into an agreement under which payments are made to the authority for the provision by the authority of childcare for a child.

(2) Subsection (1) does not apply—

(a) to childcare provided in pursuance of the duty imposed by section 7, or

(b) to childcare provided under section 18(1) or (5) of the Children Act 1989 (c. 41) (day care for children in need), provision as to charges for such care being made by section 29 of that Act.

11 Duty to assess childcare provision

(1) An English local authority must prepare assessments of the sufficiency of the provision of childcare (whether or not by them) in their area ("childcare assessments").

(2) The first childcare assessment must be prepared before the end of the period of one year beginning with the commencement of this section.

(3) Subsequent childcare assessments must be prepared at intervals not exceeding three years.

(4) The authority must keep a childcare assessment prepared by them under review until the childcare assessment is superseded by a further childcare assessment.

(5) Regulations may make provision requiring a childcare assessment—

(a) to deal with prescribed matters or be prepared according to prescribed criteria;

(b) to be in the prescribed form;

(c) to be published in the prescribed manner.

(6) In preparing a childcare assessment and keeping it under review, an English local authority must—

(a) consult such persons, or persons of such a description, as may be prescribed, and

(b) have regard to any guidance given from time to time by the Secretary of State.

(7) Subsection (5) of section 6 applies for the purposes of this section as it applies for the purposes of that section.

Information, advice and assistance

12 Duty to provide information, advice and assistance

(1) An English local authority must establish and maintain a service providing information, advice and assistance in accordance with this section.

(2) The service must provide to parents or prospective parents information which is of a prescribed description and relates to any of the following—

(a) the provision of childcare in the area of the local authority;

(b) any other services or facilities, or any publications, which may be of benefit to parents or prospective parents in their area;

(c) any other services or facilities, or any publications, which may be of benefit to children or young persons in their area.

(3) In prescribing information for the purpose of subsection (2), the Secretary of State must have regard to the needs of the parents of disabled children or young persons for information relating to—

(a) the provision of childcare which is suitable for disabled children, and

(b) other services or facilities, or publications, which may be of particular benefit to the parents of disabled children or young persons or to disabled children or young persons.

(4) The service may, in addition to providing information which it is required to provide under subsection (2), provide information relating to any of the matters mentioned in paragraphs (a) to (c) of that subsection to such persons as the local authority consider appropriate.

(5) The service must provide advice and assistance to parents or prospective parents who use, or propose to use, childcare provided in the area of the local authority.

(6) The service must be established and maintained in the manner which is best calculated to facilitate access to the service by persons in the local authority's area who may benefit from it, including, in particular, persons who might otherwise have difficulty in taking advantage of the service.

(7) In exercising their functions under this section, a local authority must have regard to any guidance given from time to time by the Secretary of State.

(8) For the purposes of this section, a child or young person is disabled if he has a disability for the purposes of the Disability Discrimination Act 1995 (c. 50).

(9) In this section—

"parent" means a parent of a child or young person and includes any individual who—

(a) has parental responsibility for a child, or

(b) has care of a child;

"prospective parent" means a pregnant woman or any other person who is likely to become, or is planning to become, a parent;

"young person" means a person who has attained the age of 18 but has not attained the age of 20.

13 Duty to provide information, advice and training to childcare providers

(1) An English local authority must, in accordance with regulations, secure the provision of information, advice and training to—

(a) persons providing childcare in their area who are registered under Part 3;

(b) persons who intend to provide childcare in their area in respect of which they will be required to be registered under Part 3;

(c) persons who provide childcare at any of the following schools in their area (whether or not they are required to be registered under Part 3)—

(i) a maintained school,

(ii) a school approved by the Secretary of State under section 342 of the Education Act 1996 (c. 56) (approval of non-maintained special schools),

(iii) an independent school;

(d) persons who intend to provide childcare at any such school (whether or not they would be required to be registered under Part 3);

(e) persons who are employed to assist any such persons as are mentioned in paragraph (a) or (c) in the provision of childcare or persons who intend to obtain such employment.

(2) An English local authority may, in addition to securing the provision of information, advice and training which they are required to secure under subsection (1), provide other information, advice and training to any persons mentioned in paragraphs (a) to (e) of that subsection.

(3) An English local authority may provide information, advice and training to persons who do not fall within any of paragraphs (a) to (e) of subsection (1) but who—

(a) provide or intend to provide childcare in their area, or

(b) are employed to assist in the provision of childcare in their area or who intend to obtain such employment.

(4) An English local authority may impose such charges as they consider reasonable for the provision of information, advice or training provided by them in pursuance of subsection (1), (2) or (3).

(5) In exercising their functions under this section, an English local authority must have regard to any guidance given from time to time by the Secretary of State.

Miscellaneous

14 Inspection

For the purposes of section 38 of the Education Act 1997 (c. 44) (inspection of local education authorities), the functions conferred on an English local authority by or under this Part are to be regarded as functions conferred on a local education authority in their capacity as such.

15 Powers of Secretary of State to secure proper performance etc.

(1) Section 496 of the 1996 Act (powers of Secretary of State to prevent unreasonable exercise of functions) applies in relation to an English local authority and the powers conferred or duties imposed on them by or under this Part as it applies in relation to a local education authority in England and the powers conferred or duties imposed on them by or under the 1996 Act.

(2) Section 497 of the 1996 Act (general default powers) applies in relation to the duties imposed on an English local authority by or for the purposes of this Part as it applies in relation to the duties imposed on a local education authority in England by or for the purposes of the 1996 Act.

(3) Section 497A of the 1996 Act (power to secure proper performance of LEA's functions) applies in relation to an English local authority's functions under this Part as it applies in relation to the functions of a local education authority in England mentioned in subsection (1) of that section.

(4) Sections 497AA and 497B of the 1996 Act apply accordingly where powers under section 497A of that Act are exercised in relation to any of the functions of an English local authority under this Part.

(5) In the application of sections 497A(2) to (7), 497AA and 497B of the 1996 Act in relation to an English local authority's functions under this Part, references to the local education authority are to be read as references to the local authority.

(6) In subsection (5) of section 497A of the 1996 Act, the reference to functions to which that section applies includes (for all purposes) functions of an English local authority under this Part.

(7) In this section, "the 1996 Act" means the Education Act 1996 (c. 56).

16 Amendments of Children Act 2004

(1) The Children Act 2004 (c. 31) is amended as follows.

(2) In section 18 (director of children's services), in subsection (2)—

(a) omit the "and" at the end of paragraph (d), and

(b) after paragraph (e) insert "; and

(f) the functions conferred on the authority under Part 1 of the Childcare Act 2006."

(3) In section 23 (interpretation), in subsection (3) (which defines "children's services")—

(a) omit the "and" at the end of paragraph (b), and

(b) after paragraph (c) insert "; and

(d) any function conferred on a local authority under Part 1 of the Childcare Act 2006."

17 Charges for early years provision at maintained school

(1) Section 451 of the Education Act 1996 (prohibition of charges for provision of education) is amended as follows.

(2) After subsection (2) insert—

"(2A) Regulations may, in relation to England, prescribe circumstances in which subsection (2) does not apply in relation to education which is early years provision (as defined by section 20 of the Childcare Act 2006) other than —

(a) early years provision provided in pursuance of the duty imposed by section 7 of that Act, or

(b) early years provision for a pupil who is of compulsory school age."

(3) In subsection (4) after paragraph (b) insert "or

(c) provided in pursuance of the duty imposed by section 7 of the Childcare Act 2006."

Interpretation

18 Meaning of childcare

(1) This section applies for the purposes of this Part and Part 3.

(2) "Childcare" means any form of care for a child and, subject to subsection (3), care includes—

(a) education for a child, and
(b) any other supervised activity for a child.

(3) "Childcare" does not include—
(a) education (or any other supervised activity) provided by a school during school hours for a registered pupil who is not a young child, or
(b) any form of health care for a child.

(4) "Childcare" does not include care provided for a child by—
(a) a parent or step-parent of the child;
(b) a person with parental responsibility for the child;
(c) a relative of the child;
(d) a person who is a local authority foster parent in relation to the child;
(e) a person who is a foster parent with whom the child has been placed by a voluntary organisation;
(f) a person who fosters the child privately.

(5) "Childcare" does not include care provided for a child if the care—
(a) is provided in any of the following establishments as part of the establishment's activities—
(i) an appropriate children's home,
(ii) a care home,
(iii) a hospital in which the child is a patient,
(iv) a residential family centre, and
(b) is so provided by the person carrying on the establishment or a person employed to work at the establishment.

(6) The reference in subsection (5)(b) to a person who is employed includes a reference to a person who is employed under a contract for services.

(7) "Childcare" does not include care provided for a child who is detained in—
(a) a young offender institution, or
(b) a secure training centre.

(8) In this section—
(a) "appropriate children's home", "local authority foster parent", "to foster a child privately" and "voluntary organisation" have the same meaning as in the Children Act 1989 (c. 41);
(b) "care home", "hospital" and "residential family centre" have the same meaning as in the Care Standards Act 2000 (c. 14);
(c) "relative", in relation to a child, means a grandparent, aunt, uncle, brother or sister, whether of the full blood or half blood or by marriage or civil partnership.

19 Meaning of "young child"

For the purposes of this Part and Part 3, a child is a "young child" during the period—
(a) beginning with his birth, and
(b) ending immediately before the 1st September next following the date on which he attains the age of five.

20 Meaning of "early years provision"

In this Part "early years provision" means the provision of childcare for a young child.

21 Interpretation of Part 1

In this Part—

"childcare" has the meaning given by section 18;

"early years provision" has the meaning given by section 20;

"prescribed" means prescribed by regulations;

"regulations" means regulations made by the Secretary of State;

"young child" has the meaning given by section 19.

PART 2

GENERAL FUNCTIONS OF LOCAL AUTHORITY: WALES

Provision of childcare

22 Duty to secure sufficient childcare for working parents

(1) A Welsh local authority must secure, so far as is reasonably practicable, that the provision of childcare (whether or not by them) is sufficient to meet the requirements of parents in their area who require childcare in order to enable them—

(a) to take up, or remain in, work, or

(b) to undertake education or training which could reasonably be expected to assist them to obtain work.

(2) In determining for the purposes of subsection (1) whether the provision of childcare is sufficient to meet those requirements, a local authority—

(a) must have regard to the needs of parents in their area for—

(i) the provision of childcare in respect of which the child care element of working tax credit is payable,

(ii) the provision of childcare which is suitable for disabled children, and

(iii) the provision of childcare involving the use of the Welsh language, and

(b) may have regard to any childcare which they expect to be available outside their area.

(3) In discharging their duty under subsection (1), a local authority must have regard to any guidance given from time to time by the Assembly.

(4) The Assembly may by order amend subsection (2) (and subsection (6) so far as relating to that subsection) so as to modify the matters to which a local authority must or may have regard in determining whether the provision of childcare is sufficient.

(5) Except in relation to a disabled child, this section does not apply in relation to childcare for a child on or after the 1st September next following the date on which he attains the age of 14.

(6) In this section—

"child care element", in relation to working tax credit, is to be read in accordance with section 12 of the Tax Credits Act 2002 (c. 21);

"disabled child" means a child who has a disability for the purposes of the Disability Discrimination Act 1995 (c. 50);

"parent" includes any individual who—

(a) has parental responsibility for a child, or

(b) has care of a child.

23 Powers of local authority in relation to the provision of childcare

(1) A Welsh local authority may—

(a) assist any person who provides or proposes to provide childcare;

(b) make arrangements with any other person for the provision of childcare;

(c) provide childcare.

(2) The assistance which a local authority may give under subsection (1)(a) includes financial assistance; and the arrangements which a local authority may make under subsection (1)(b) include arrangements involving the provision of financial assistance by the authority.

(3) In exercising their functions under this section, a Welsh local authority must have regard to any guidance given from time to time by the Assembly.

24 Arrangements between local authority and childcare providers

(1) This section applies where a Welsh local authority make arrangements with a person (other than the governing body of a maintained school) for the provision by that person of childcare in consideration of financial assistance provided by the authority under the arrangements.

(2) The local authority must exercise their functions with a view to securing that the provider of the childcare meets any requirements imposed on him by the arrangements.

(3) The requirements imposed by the arrangements may, in particular, if any specified conditions are not satisfied, require the repayment of the whole or any part of any financial assistance provided by the local authority under the arrangements.

25 Charges where local authority provide childcare

(1) A Welsh local authority may enter into an agreement under which payments are made to the authority for the provision by the authority of childcare for a child.

(2) Subsection (1) does not apply to childcare provided under section 18 of the Children Act 1989 (c. 41) (day care for pre-school and other children), provision as to charges for such care being made by section 29 of that Act.

26 Power to require local authority to assess childcare provision

(1) The Assembly may by regulations require a Welsh local authority to—

(a) prepare assessments at prescribed intervals of the sufficiency of the provision of childcare (whether or not by them) in their area;

(b) review any such assessment prepared by them.

(2) Regulations under subsection (1) may make provision for the manner in which an assessment or review is to be prepared and, in particular, may require the local authority to—

(a) consult such persons, or persons of such a description, as may be prescribed, and

(b) have regard to any guidance given from time to time by the Assembly.

(3) Subsection (5) of section 22 applies for the purposes of this section as it applies for the purposes of that section.

Information, advice and assistance

27 Duty to provide information, advice and assistance

(1) A Welsh local authority must establish and maintain a service providing information, advice and assistance in accordance with this section.

(2) The service must provide to parents or prospective parents information which is of a prescribed description and relates to any of the following—

(a) the provision of childcare in the area of the local authority;

(b) any other services or facilities, or any publications, which may be of benefit to parents or prospective parents in their area;

(c) any other services or facilities, or any publications, which may be of benefit to children or young persons in their area.

(3) In prescribing information for the purpose of subsection (2), the Assembly must have regard to the needs of the parents of disabled children or young persons for information relating to—

(a) the provision of childcare which is suitable for disabled children, and

(b) other services or facilities, or publications, which may be of particular benefit to the parents of disabled children or young persons or to disabled children or young persons.

(4) The service may, in addition to providing information which it is required to provide under subsection (2), provide information relating to any of the matters mentioned in paragraphs (a) to (c) of that subsection to such persons as the local authority consider appropriate.

(5) The service must provide advice and assistance to parents or prospective parents who use, or propose to use, childcare provided in the area of the local authority.

(6) The service must be established and maintained in the manner which is best calculated to facilitate access to the service by persons in the local authority's area who may benefit from it, including, in particular, persons who might otherwise have difficulty in taking advantage of the service.

(7) In exercising their functions under this section, a local authority must have regard to any guidance given from time to time by the Assembly.

(8) For the purposes of this section, a child or young person is disabled if he has a disability for the purposes of the Disability Discrimination Act 1995 (c. 50).

(9) In this section—

"parent" means a parent of a child or young person and includes any individual who—

(a) has parental responsibility for a child, or

(b) has care of a child;

"prospective parent" means a pregnant woman or any other person who is likely to become, or is planning to become, a parent;

"young person" means a person who has attained the age of 18 but has not attained the age of 20.

Miscellaneous

28 Inspection

For the purposes of section 38 of the Education Act 1997 (c. 44) (inspection of local education authorities), the functions conferred on a Welsh local authority by or under this Part are to be regarded as functions conferred on a local education authority in their capacity as such.

29 Powers of Assembly to secure proper performance etc.

(1) Section 496 of the 1996 Act (power to prevent unreasonable exercise of functions) applies in relation to a Welsh local authority and the powers conferred or duties imposed on them by or under this Part as it applies in relation to a local education authority in Wales and the powers conferred or duties imposed on them by or under the 1996 Act.

(2) Section 497 of the 1996 Act (general default powers) applies in relation to the duties imposed on a Welsh local authority by or for the purposes of this Part as it applies in relation to the duties imposed on a local education authority in Wales by or for the purposes of the 1996 Act.

(3) Section 497A of the 1996 Act (power to secure proper performance of LEA's functions) applies in relation to a Welsh local authority's functions under this Part as it applies in relation to the functions of a local education authority in Wales mentioned in subsection (1) of that section.

(4) Sections 497AA and 497B of the 1996 Act apply accordingly where powers under section 497A of that Act are exercised in relation to any of the functions of a Welsh local authority under this Part.

(5) In the application of sections 497A(2) to (7), 497AA and 497B of the 1996 Act in relation to a Welsh local authority's functions under this Part, references to the local education authority are to be read as references to the local authority.

(6) In subsection (5) of section 497A of the 1996 Act, the reference to functions to which that section applies includes (for all purposes) functions of a Welsh local authority under this Part.

(7) In this section, "the 1996 Act" means the Education Act 1996 (c. 56).

Interpretation

30 Interpretation of Part 2

In this Part—

"childcare" means—

(a) child minding or day care within the meaning of Part 10A of the Children Act 1989 (c. 41) in respect of which the provider is required to be registered under that Part;

(b) care provided by a person of a description approved in accordance with a scheme made by the Assembly under section 12(5) of the Tax Credits Act 2002 (c. 21);

"prescribed" means prescribed by regulations made by the Assembly.

PART 3

REGULATION OF PROVISION OF CHILDCARE IN ENGLAND

CHAPTER 1

GENERAL FUNCTIONS OF CHIEF INSPECTOR

31 General functions of the Chief Inspector

(1) The Chief Inspector has the general duty of keeping the Secretary of State informed about—

(a) the contribution of regulated early years provision in England to the well-being of children for whom it is provided;

(b) the quality and standards of regulated early years provision in England;

(c) how far regulated early years provision in England meets the needs of the range of children for whom it is provided;

(d) the quality of leadership and management in connection with regulated early years provision in England.

(2) In subsection (1), "regulated early years provision" means early years provision in respect of which a person is required to be registered under Chapter 2 or in respect of which he would be required to be registered under that Chapter but for section 34(2) (exemption for provision for children aged 3 or over at certain schools).

(3) When asked to do so by the Secretary of State, the Chief Inspector must give advice to the Secretary of State on such matters relating to early years provision or later years provision in England as may be specified in the Secretary of State's request.

(4) The Chief Inspector may at any time give advice to the Secretary of State on any matter connected with—

(a) early years provision or later years provision in England generally, or

(b) early years provision or later years provision in England by particular persons or on particular premises.

(5) The Chief Inspector is to have such other functions in connection with early years provision or later years provision in England as may be assigned to him by the Secretary of State.

32 Maintenance of the two childcare registers

(1) The Chief Inspector must maintain two registers.

(2) The first register ("the early years register") is to be a register of all persons who are registered as early years childminders or other early years providers under Chapter 2 (which provides for the compulsory registration of persons providing early years provision).

(3) The second register ("the general childcare register") is to be divided into two Parts.

(4) The first Part ("Part A") is to be a register of all persons who are registered as later years childminders or other later years providers under Chapter 3 (which provides for the compulsory registration of persons providing later years provision for children under the age of eight).

(5) The second Part ("Part B") is to be a register of all persons who are registered as childminders or other childcare providers under Chapter 4 (which provides for the voluntary registration of persons providing early years provision or later years provision in respect of which they are not required to be registered under Chapter 2 or 3).

CHAPTER 2

REGULATION OF EARLY YEARS PROVISION

Requirements to register

33 Requirement to register: early years childminders

(1) A person may not provide early years childminding in England unless he is registered in the early years register as an early years childminder.

(2) The Secretary of State may by order provide that, in circumstances specified in the order, subsection (1) does not apply in relation to early years childminding.

(3) The circumstances specified in an order under subsection (2) may relate to one or more of the following matters (among others)—

- (a) the person providing the early years childminding;
- (b) the child or children for whom it is provided;
- (c) the nature of the early years childminding;
- (d) the premises on which it is provided;
- (e) the times during which it is provided;
- (f) the arrangements under which it is provided.

(4) If it appears to the Chief Inspector that a person has provided early years childminding in contravention of subsection (1), he may serve a notice ("an enforcement notice") on the person.

(5) An enforcement notice may be served on a person—

(a) by delivering it to him, or

(b) by sending it by post.

(6) An enforcement notice has effect until it is revoked by the Chief Inspector.

(7) A person commits an offence if, at any time when an enforcement notice has effect in relation to him and without reasonable excuse, he provides early years childminding in contravention of subsection (1).

(8) A person guilty of an offence under subsection (7) is liable on summary conviction to a fine not exceeding level 5 on the standard scale.

34 Requirement to register: other early years providers

(1) A person may not provide—

(a) early years provision on premises in England which are not domestic premises, or

(b) early years provision on domestic premises in England which would be early years childminding but for section 96(5),

unless he is registered in the early years register in respect of the premises.

(2) Subsection (1) does not apply in relation to early years provision for a child or children who has (or have) attained the age of three if—

(a) the provision is made at any of the following schools as part of the school's activities—

(i) a maintained school,

(ii) a school approved by the Secretary of State under section 342 of the Education Act 1996 (c. 56) (approval of non-maintained special schools), or

(iii) an independent school,

(b) the provision is made by the proprietor of the school or a person employed to work at the school, and

(c) the child is a registered pupil at the school or, if the provision is made for more than one child, at least one of the children is a registered pupil at the school.

(3) The Secretary of State may by order provide that, in circumstances specified in the order, subsection (1) does not apply in relation to early years provision.

(4) The circumstances specified in an order under subsection (3) may relate to one or more of the following matters (among others)—

(a) the person providing the early years provision;

(b) the child or children for whom it is provided;

(c) the nature of the early years provision;

(d) the premises on which it is provided;

(e) the times during which it is provided;

(f) the arrangements under which it is provided.

(5) A person commits an offence if, without reasonable excuse, he provides early years provision in contravention of subsection (1).

(6) A person guilty of an offence under subsection (5) is liable on summary conviction to a fine not exceeding level 5 on the standard scale.

Process of registration

35 Applications for registration: early years childminders

(1) A person who proposes to provide early years childminding in respect of which he is required by section 33(1) to be registered may make an application to the Chief Inspector for registration as an early years childminder.

(2) An application under subsection (1) must—

(a) give any prescribed information about prescribed matters,

(b) give any other information which the Chief Inspector reasonably requires the applicant to give, and

(c) be accompanied by any prescribed fee.

(3) The Chief Inspector must grant an application under subsection (1) if—

(a) the applicant is not disqualified from registration by regulations under section 75, and

(b) it appears to the Chief Inspector that any requirements prescribed for the purposes of this subsection ("the prescribed requirements for registration") are satisfied and are likely to continue to be satisfied.

(4) The Chief Inspector must refuse any application under subsection (1) which subsection (3) does not require him to grant.

(5) The prescribed requirements for registration may include requirements relating to—

(a) the applicant;

(b) the premises on which the early years childminding is to be provided;

(c) the arrangements for early years childminding on those premises;

(d) any person who may be caring for children on those premises;

(e) any other person who may be on those premises.

36 Applications for registration: other early years providers

(1) A person who proposes to provide on any premises early years provision in respect of which he is required by section 34(1) to be registered may make an application to the Chief Inspector for registration as an early years provider in respect of the premises.

(2) An application under subsection (1) must—

(a) give any prescribed information about prescribed matters,

(b) give any other information which the Chief Inspector reasonably requires the applicant to give, and

(c) be accompanied by any prescribed fee.

(3) The Chief Inspector must grant an application under subsection (1) if—

(a) the applicant is not disqualified from registration by regulations under section 75, and

(b) it appears to the Chief Inspector that any requirements prescribed for the purposes of this subsection ("the prescribed requirements for registration") are satisfied and are likely to continue to be satisfied.

(4) The Chief Inspector must refuse any application under subsection (1) which subsection (3) does not require him to grant.

(5) The prescribed requirements for registration may include requirements relating to—
(a) the applicant;
(b) the premises on which the early years provision is to be provided;
(c) the arrangements for early years provision on those premises;
(d) any person who may be caring for children on those premises;
(e) any other person who may be on those premises.

37 Entry on the register and certificates

(1) If an application under section 35(1) is granted, the Chief Inspector must—
(a) register the applicant in the early years register as an early years childminder, and
(b) give the applicant a certificate of registration stating that he is so registered.

(2) If an application under section 36(1) is granted, the Chief Inspector must—
(a) register the applicant in the early years register as an early years provider other than a childminder, in respect of the premises in question, and
(b) give the applicant a certificate of registration stating that he is so registered.

(3) A certificate of registration given to the applicant in pursuance of subsection (1) or (2) must contain prescribed information about prescribed matters.

(4) If there is a change of circumstances which requires the amendment of a certificate of registration, the Chief Inspector must give the registered early years provider an amended certificate.

(5) If the Chief Inspector is satisfied that a certificate of registration has been lost or destroyed, the Chief Inspector must give the registered early years provider a copy, on payment by the provider of any prescribed fee.

38 Conditions on registration

(1) The Chief Inspector may impose such conditions as he thinks fit on the registration of an early years provider under this Chapter.

(2) The power conferred by subsection (1) may be exercised at the time when the Chief Inspector registers the person in pursuance of section 37 or at any subsequent time.

(3) The Chief Inspector may at any time vary or remove any condition imposed under subsection (1).

(4) The power conferred by subsection (1) includes power to impose conditions for the purpose of giving effect to an order under subsection (1)(a) of section 39 or regulations under subsection (1)(b) of that section.

(5) An early years provider registered under this Chapter commits an offence if, without reasonable excuse, he fails to comply with any condition imposed under subsection (1).

(6) A person guilty of an offence under subsection (5) is liable on summary conviction to a fine not exceeding level 5 on the standard scale.

Requirements to be met by early years providers

39 The Early Years Foundation Stage

(1) For the purpose of promoting the well-being of young children for whom early years provision is provided by early years providers to whom section 40 applies, the Secretary of State must—

(a) by order specify in accordance with section 41 such requirements as he considers appropriate relating to learning by, and the development of, such children ("learning and development requirements"), and

(b) by regulations specify in accordance with section 43 such requirements as he considers appropriate governing the activities of early years providers to whom section 40 applies ("welfare requirements").

(2) The learning and development requirements and the welfare requirements are together to be known as "the Early Years Foundation Stage".

40 Duty to implement Early Years Foundation Stage

(1) This section applies to—

(a) early years providers providing early years provision in respect of which they are registered under this Chapter, and

(b) early years providers providing early years provision in respect of which, but for section 34(2) (exemption for provision for children aged 3 or over at certain schools), they would be required to be registered under this Chapter.

(2) An early years provider to whom this section applies—

(a) must secure that the early years provision meets the learning and development requirements, and

(b) must comply with the welfare requirements.

41 The learning and development requirements

(1) The learning and development requirements must cover the areas of learning and development specified in subsection (3).

(2) The learning and development requirements may specify in relation to each of the areas of learning and development—

(a) the knowledge, skills and understanding which young children of different abilities and maturities are expected to have before the 1st September next following the day on which they attain the age of five ("early learning goals");

(b) the matters, skills and processes which are required to be taught to young children of different abilities and maturities ("educational programmes"), and

(c) the arrangements which are required for assessing children for the purpose of ascertaining what they have achieved in relation to the early learning goals ("assessment arrangements").

(3) The areas of learning and development are as follows—

(a) personal, social and emotional development,

(b) communication, language and literacy,

(c) problem solving, reasoning and numeracy,

(d) knowledge and understanding of the world,

(e) physical development, and

(f) creative development.

(4) The Secretary of State may by order amend subsection (3).

(5) A learning and development order may not require—

(a) the allocation of any particular period or periods of time to the teaching of any educational programme or any matter, skill or process forming part of it, or

(b) the making in the timetables of any early years provider of provision of any particular kind for the periods to be allocated to such teaching.

(6) In this section "a learning and development order" means an order under section 39(1)(a).

42 Further provisions about assessment arrangements

(1) A learning and development order specifying assessment arrangements may confer or impose on any of the persons mentioned in subsection (2) such functions as appear to the Secretary of State to be required.

(2) Those persons are—

(a) an early years provider,

(b) the governing body or head teacher of a maintained school in England, and

(c) an English local authority.

(3) A learning and development order may specify such assessment arrangements as may for the time being be made by a person specified in the order.

(4) Provision must be made for determining the extent to which any assessment arrangements, and the implementation of the arrangements, achieve the purpose for which the arrangements were made; and any such provision may be made by or under the learning and development order specifying the arrangements or (where the order specifies the person making the arrangements) in the arrangements themselves.

(5) The duties that may be imposed by virtue of subsection (1) include, in relation to persons exercising any power in pursuance of provision made by virtue of subsection (4), the duty to permit them—

(a) to enter premises on which the early years provision is provided,

(b) to observe implementation of the arrangements, and

(c) to inspect, and take copies of, documents and other articles.

(6) A learning and development order specifying assessment arrangements may authorise the making of such provisions giving full effect to or otherwise supplementing the provisions made by the order (other than provision conferring or imposing functions

as mentioned in subsection (1)) as appear to the Secretary of State to be expedient; and any provisions made under such an order, on being published as specified in the order, are to have effect for the purposes of this Chapter as if made by the order.

(7) In this section "a learning and development order" means an order under section 39(1)(a).

43 Welfare requirements

(1) The matters that may be dealt with by welfare regulations include—

(a) the welfare of the children concerned;

(b) the arrangements for safeguarding the children concerned;

(c) suitability of persons to care for, or be in regular contact with, the children concerned;

(d) qualifications and training;

(e) the suitability of premises and equipment;

(f) the manner in which the early years provision is organised;

(g) procedures for dealing with complaints;

(h) the keeping of records;

(i) the provision of information.

(2) Before making welfare regulations, the Secretary of State must consult the Chief Inspector and any other persons he considers appropriate.

(3) Welfare regulations may provide—

(a) that a person who without reasonable excuse fails to comply with any requirement of the regulations is guilty of an offence, and

(b) that a person guilty of the offence is liable on summary conviction to a fine not exceeding level 5 on the standard scale.

(4) In this section "welfare regulations" means regulations under section 39(1)(b).

44 Instruments specifying learning and development or welfare requirements

(1) A relevant instrument may, instead of containing the provisions to be made, refer to provisions in a document published as specified in the instrument and direct that those provisions are to have effect or, as the case may be, are to have effect as specified in the instrument.

(2) The power to make a relevant instrument may be exercised so as to confer powers or impose duties on the Chief Inspector in the exercise of his functions under this Part.

(3) In particular, that power may be exercised so as to require or authorise the Chief Inspector, in exercising those functions, to have regard to factors, standards and other matters prescribed by or referred to in the instrument.

(4) If a relevant instrument requires any person (other than the Chief Inspector) to have regard to or meet factors, standards and other matters prescribed by or referred to in the instrument, the instrument may also provide for any allegation that the person has failed to do so to be taken into account—

(a) by the Chief Inspector in the exercise of his functions under this Part, or

(b) in any proceedings under this Part.

(5) In this section "a relevant instrument" means an order under subsection (1)(a) of section 39 or regulations under subsection (1)(b) of that section.

45 Procedure for making certain orders

(1) This section applies where the Secretary of State proposes to make an order under section 39(1)(a) specifying early learning goals or educational programmes.

(2) The Secretary of State must give notice of the proposal—

(a) to such bodies representing the interests of early years providers as the Secretary of State considers appropriate, and

(b) to any other persons with whom consultation appears to the Secretary of State to be desirable,

and must give them a reasonable opportunity of submitting evidence and representations as to the issues arising.

(3) When the Secretary of State has considered any evidence and representations submitted to him in pursuance of subsection (2), he must publish in such manner as, in his opinion, is likely to bring them to the notice of persons having a special interest in early years provision—

(a) a draft of the proposed order and any associated document, and

(b) a summary of the views expressed during the consultation.

(4) The Secretary of State must allow a period of not less than one month beginning with the publication of the draft of the proposed order for the submission of any further evidence and representations as to the issues arising.

(5) When the period so allowed has expired, the Secretary of State may make the order, with or without modifications.

46 Power to enable exemptions to be conferred

(1) Regulations may enable the Secretary of State, in prescribed circumstances, to direct in respect of a particular early years provider or a particular description of early years providers, that to such extent as may be prescribed the learning and development requirements—

(a) do not apply, or

(b) apply with such modifications as may be specified in the direction.

(2) Regulations may enable an early years provider, in prescribed circumstances, to determine in respect of a particular young child that to such extent as may be prescribed the learning and development requirements—

(a) do not apply, or

(b) apply with such modifications as may be specified in the determination.

47 Independent schools

(1) In section 157 of the Education Act 2002 (c. 32) (independent school standards) after subsection (1) insert—

"(1A) In relation to England, the standards do not apply to early years provision for pupils who have not attained the age of three (separate requirements as to such provision being imposed by or under Part 3 of the Childcare Act 2006)."

(2) For subsection (2) of that section substitute—

"(2) In this Chapter "independent school standards" means—

(a) the standards for the time being prescribed under this section, and

(b) in relation to early years provision in England for pupils who have attained the age of three, the Early Years Foundation Stage."

(3) In section 171 of that Act (interpretation of Chapter 1 of Part 10), after the definition of "Chief Inspector" insert—

"“early years provision”, in relation to England, has the meaning given by section 96(2) of the Childcare Act 2006;".

48 Amendments relating to curriculum

Schedule 1 (which contains amendments relating to the preceding provisions of this Chapter, including amendments excluding or modifying the application to early years provision of provisions of Part 6 of the Education Act 2002 (c. 32)) has effect.

Inspection

49 Inspections

(1) This section applies to early years provision in respect of which the early years provider is registered under this Chapter.

(2) The Chief Inspector—

(a) must at such intervals as may be prescribed inspect early years provision to which this section applies,

(b) must inspect early years provision to which this section applies at any time when the Secretary of State requires the Chief Inspector to secure its inspection, and

(c) may inspect early years provision to which this section applies at any other time when the Chief Inspector considers that it would be appropriate for it to be inspected.

(3) Regulations may provide that in prescribed circumstances the Chief Inspector is not required to inspect early years provision at an interval prescribed for the purposes of subsection (2)(a).

(4) Regulations may provide that the Chief Inspector is not required by subsection (2)(a) to inspect early years provision at an independent school if the early years provision is inspected in prescribed circumstances by a body approved by the Secretary of State for the purposes of this subsection.

(5) A requirement made by the Secretary of State as mentioned in subsection (2)(b) may be imposed in relation to early years provision at particular premises or a class of premises.

(6) Regulations may make provision requiring the registered person to notify prescribed persons of the fact that early years provision is to be inspected under this section.

(7) If the Chief Inspector so elects in the case of an inspection falling within paragraph (b) or (c) of subsection (2), that inspection is to be treated as if it were an inspection falling within paragraph (a) of that subsection.

50 Report of inspections

(1) After conducting an inspection under section 49, the Chief Inspector must make a report in writing on—

(a) the contribution of the early years provision to the well-being of the children for whom it is provided,

(b) the quality and standards of the early years provision,

(c) how far the early years provision meets the needs of the range of children for whom it is provided, and

(d) the quality of leadership and management in connection with the early years provision.

(2) The Chief Inspector—

(a) may send a copy of the report to the Secretary of State and must do so without delay if the Secretary of State requests a copy,

(b) must ensure that a copy of the report is sent without delay to the registered person, 23

(c) must ensure that copies of the report, or such parts of it as he considers appropriate, are sent to such other persons as may be prescribed, and

(d) may arrange for the report (or parts of it) to be further published in any manner he considers appropriate.

(3) Regulations may make provision—

(a) requiring the registered person to make a copy of any report sent to him under subsection (2)(b) available for inspection by prescribed persons;

(b) requiring the registered person, except in prescribed cases, to provide a copy of the report to prescribed persons;

(c) authorising the registered person in prescribed cases to charge a fee for providing a copy of the report.

(4) Subsections (2) to (4) of section 11 of the Education Act 2005 (c. 18) (publication of inspection reports) apply in relation to the publication of a report under subsection (2) of this section as they apply in relation to the publication of a report under any of the provisions mentioned in subsection (2) of section 11.

Interpretation

51 Interpretation of Chapter 2

In this Chapter—

"assessment arrangements" is to be read in accordance with section 41(2)(c);

"early learning goals" is to be read in accordance with section 41(2)(a);

"educational programmes" is to be read in accordance with section 41(2)(b);

"learning and development requirements" means requirements specified by order under section 39(1)(a);

"welfare requirements" means requirements specified by regulations under section 39(1)(b).

CHAPTER 3

REGULATION OF LATER YEARS PROVISION FOR CHILDREN UNDER 8

Requirements to register

52 Requirement to register: later years childminders for children under eight

(1) A person may not provide later years childminding in England for a child who has not attained the age of eight unless he is registered in Part A of the general childcare register as a childminder.

(2) The Secretary of State may by order provide that, in circumstances specified in the order, subsection (1) does not apply in relation to later years childminding.

(3) The circumstances specified in an order under subsection (2) may relate to one or more of the following matters (among others)—

- (a) the person providing the later years childminding;
- (b) the child or children for whom it is provided;
- (c) the nature of the later years childminding;
- (d) the premises on which it is provided;
- (e) the times during which it is provided;
- (f) the arrangements under which it is provided.

(4) If it appears to the Chief Inspector that a person has provided later years childminding in contravention of subsection (1), the Chief Inspector may serve a notice ("an enforcement notice") on the person.

(5) An enforcement notice may be served on a person—

- (a) by delivering it to him, or
- (b) by sending it by post.

(6) An enforcement notice has effect until it is revoked by the Chief Inspector.

(7) A person commits an offence if, at any time when an enforcement notice has effect in relation to him and without reasonable excuse, he provides later years childminding in contravention of subsection (1).

(8) A person guilty of an offence under subsection (7) is liable on summary conviction to a fine not exceeding level 5 on the standard scale.

53 Requirement to register: other later years providers for children under eight

(1) A person may not provide for a child who has not attained the age of eight—

- (a) later years provision on premises in England which are not domestic premises, or

(b) later years provision on domestic premises in England which would be later years childminding but for section 96(9),

unless he is registered in Part A of the general childcare register in respect of the premises.

(2) Subsection (1) does not apply in relation to later years provision for a child if—

(a) the provision is made at any of the following schools as part of the school's activities—

(i) a maintained school,

(ii) a school approved by the Secretary of State under section 342 of the Education Act 1996 (c. 56) (approval of non-maintained special schools), or

(iii) an independent school,

(b) the provision is made by the proprietor of the school or a person employed to work at the school, and

(c) the child is a registered pupil at the school or, if the provision is made for more than one child who has not attained the age of eight, at least one of the children is a registered pupil at the school.

(3) The Secretary of State may by order provide that, in circumstances specified in the order, subsection (1) does not apply in relation to later years provision.

(4) The circumstances specified in an order under subsection (3) may relate to one or more of the following matters (among others)—

(a) the person providing the later years provision;

(b) the child or children for whom it is provided;

(c) the nature of the later years provision;

(d) the premises on which it is provided;

(e) the times during which it is provided;

(f) the arrangements under which it is provided.

(5) A person commits an offence if, without reasonable excuse, he provides later years provision in contravention of subsection (1).

(6) A person guilty of an offence under subsection (5) is liable on summary conviction to a fine not exceeding level 5 on the standard scale.

Process of registration

54 Applications for registration: later years childminders

(1) A person who proposes to provide later years childminding in respect of which he is required by section 52(1) to be registered may make an application to the Chief Inspector for registration as a later years childminder.

(2) An application under subsection (1) must—

(a) give any prescribed information about prescribed matters,

(b) give any other information which the Chief Inspector reasonably requires the applicant to give, and

(c) be accompanied by any prescribed fee.

(3) The Chief Inspector must grant an application under subsection (1) if—

(a) the applicant is not disqualified from registration by regulations under section 75, and

(b) it appears to the Chief Inspector that any requirements prescribed for the purposes of this subsection ("the prescribed requirements for registration") are satisfied and are likely to continue to be satisfied.

(4) The Chief Inspector must refuse any application under subsection (1) which subsection (3) does not require him to grant.

(5) The prescribed requirements for registration may include requirements relating to—

(a) the applicant;

(b) the premises on which the later years childminding is to be provided;

(c) the arrangements for later years childminding on those premises;

(d) any person who may be caring for children on those premises;

(e) any other person who may be on those premises.

55 Applications for registration: other later years providers

(1) A person who proposes to provide on any premises later years provision in respect of which he is required by section 53(1) to be registered may make an application to the Chief Inspector for registration as a later years provider in respect of the premises.

(2) An application under subsection (1) must—

(a) give any prescribed information about prescribed matters,

(b) give any other information which the Chief Inspector reasonably requires the applicant to give, and

(c) be accompanied by any prescribed fee.

(3) The Chief Inspector must grant an application under subsection (1) if—

(a) the applicant is not disqualified from registration by regulations under section 75, and

(b) it appears to the Chief Inspector that any requirements prescribed for the purposes of this subsection ("the prescribed requirements for registration") are satisfied and are likely to continue to be satisfied.

(4) The Chief Inspector must refuse any application under subsection (1) which subsection (3) does not require him to grant.

(5) The prescribed requirements for registration may include requirements relating to—

(a) the applicant;

(b) the premises on which the later years provision is to be provided;

(c) the arrangements for later years provision on those premises;

(d) any person who may be caring for children on those premises;

(e) any other person who may be on those premises.

56 Entry on the register and certificates

(1) If an application under section 54(1) is granted, the Chief Inspector must—

(a) register the applicant in Part A of the general childcare register as a later years childminder, and

(b) give the applicant a certificate of registration stating that he is so registered.

(2) If an application under section 55(1) is granted, the Chief Inspector must—

(a) register the applicant in Part A of the general childcare register as a later years provider other than a childminder, in respect of the premises in question, and

(b) give the applicant a certificate of registration stating that he is so registered.

(3) A certificate of registration given to the applicant in pursuance of subsection (1) or (2) must contain prescribed information about prescribed matters.

(4) If there is a change of circumstances which requires the amendment of a certificate of registration, the Chief Inspector must give the registered later years provider an amended certificate.

(5) If the Chief Inspector is satisfied that a certificate of registration has been lost or destroyed, the Chief Inspector must give the registered later years provider a copy, on payment by the provider of any prescribed fee.

57 Special procedure for registered early years providers

(1) If a person who is registered in the early years register as an early years childminder gives notice to the Chief Inspector that he proposes to provide later years childminding in respect of which he is required to be registered under this Chapter, the Chief Inspector must—

(a) register the person in Part A of the general childcare register as a later years childminder, and

(b) give the person a certificate of registration stating that he is so registered.

(2) If a person who is registered in the early years register in respect of particular premises as an early years provider other than a childminder gives notice to the Chief Inspector that he proposes to provide later years provision in respect of which he is required to be registered under this Chapter on the same premises, the Chief Inspector must—

(a) register the person in Part A of the general childcare register as a later years provider other than a childminder, in respect of the premises, and

(b) give the person a certificate of registration stating that he is so registered.

(3) Subsections (3) to (5) of section 56 apply in relation to a certificate of registration given in pursuance of subsection (1) or (2) of this section as they apply in relation to a certificate of registration given in pursuance of subsection (1) or (2) of that section.

Regulation

58 Conditions on registration

(1) The Chief Inspector may impose such conditions as he thinks fit on the registration of a later years provider under this Chapter.

(2) The power conferred by subsection (1) may be exercised at the time when the Chief Inspector registers the person in pursuance of section 56 or 57 or at any subsequent time.

(3) The Chief Inspector may at any time vary or remove any condition imposed under subsection (1).

(4) The power conferred by subsection (1) includes power to impose conditions for the purpose of giving effect to regulations under section 59.

(5) A later years provider registered under this Chapter commits an offence if, without reasonable excuse, he fails to comply with any condition imposed under subsection (1).

(6) A person guilty of an offence under subsection (5) is liable on summary conviction to a fine not exceeding level 5 on the standard scale.

59 Regulations governing activities

(1) This section applies to—

(a) later years providers providing later years provision in respect of which they are registered under this Chapter, and

(b) later years providers providing later years provision in respect of which, but for section 53(2) (exemption for provision for children at certain schools), they would be required to be registered under this Chapter.

(2) The Secretary of State may, after consulting the Chief Inspector and any other person he considers appropriate, make regulations governing the activities of later years providers to whom this section applies.

(3) The regulations may deal with the following matters (among others)—

(a) the welfare of the children concerned;

(b) the arrangements for safeguarding the children concerned;

(c) suitability of persons to care for, or be in regular contact with, the children concerned;

(d) qualifications and training;

(e) the suitability of premises and equipment;

(f) the manner in which the later years provision is organised;

(g) procedures for dealing with complaints;

(h) the keeping of records;

(i) the provision of information.

(4) The power to make regulations under this section may be exercised so as confer powers or impose duties on the Chief Inspector in the exercise of his functions under this Part.

(5) In particular, it may be so exercised so as to require the Chief Inspector, in exercising his functions under this Part, to have regard to factors, standards and other matters prescribed by or referred to in the regulations.

(6) If the regulations require any person (other than the Chief Inspector) to have regard to or to meet factors, standards and other matters prescribed by or referred to in the regulations, they may also provide for any allegation that the person has failed to do so to be taken into account—

(a) by the Chief Inspector in the exercise of his functions under this Part, or

(b) in any proceedings under this Part.

(7) The regulations may provide—

(a) that a person who without reasonable excuse fails to comply with any requirement of the regulations is guilty of an offence, and

(b) that a person guilty of the offence is liable on summary conviction to a fine not exceeding level 5 on the standard scale.

Inspection

60 Inspections

(1) This section applies to later years provision in respect of which the provider is registered under this Chapter.

(2) The Chief Inspector—

(a) must inspect later years provision to which this section applies at any time when the Secretary of State requires the Chief Inspector to secure its inspection, and

(b) may inspect later years provision to which this section applies at any other time when the Chief Inspector considers that it would be appropriate for it to be inspected.

(3) A requirement made by the Secretary of State as mentioned in subsection (2)(a) may be imposed in relation to later years provision at particular premises or a class of premises.

(4) Regulations may make provision requiring the registered person to notify prescribed persons of the fact that later years provision is to be inspected under this section.

61 Report of inspections

(1) After conducting an inspection under section 60, the Chief Inspector may make a report in writing on such of the following matters as he considers appropriate—

(a) the contribution of the later years provision to the well-being of the children for whom it is provided,

(b) the quality and standards of the later years provision,

(c) how far the later years provision meets the needs of the range of children for whom it is provided, and

(d) the quality of leadership and management in connection with the later years provision.

(2) The Chief Inspector—

(a) may send a copy of the report to the Secretary of State and must do so without delay if the Secretary of State requests a copy,

(b) must ensure that a copy of the report is sent without delay to the registered person,

(c) must ensure that copies of the report, or such parts of it as he considers appropriate, are sent to such other persons as may be prescribed, and

(d) may arrange for the report (or parts of it) to be further published in any manner he considers appropriate.

(3) Regulations may make provision—

(a) requiring the registered person to make a copy of any report sent to him under subsection (2)(b) available for inspection by prescribed persons;

(b) requiring the registered person, except in prescribed cases, to provide a copy of the report to prescribed persons;

(c) authorising the registered person in prescribed cases to charge a fee for providing a copy of the report.

(4) Subsections (2) to (4) of section 11 of the Education Act 2005 (c. 18)(publication of inspection reports) apply in relation to the publication of a report under subsection (2) of this section as they apply in relation to the publication of a report under any of the provisions mentioned in subsection (2) of section 11.

CHAPTER 4

VOLUNTARY REGISTRATION

Process of voluntary registration

62 Applications for registration on the general register: childminders

(1) A person who provides or proposes to provide in England—

(a) later years childminding for a child who has attained the age of eight, or

(b) early years childminding or later years childminding for a child who has not attained that age but in respect of which the person is not required to be registered under Chapter 2 or 3,

may make an application to the Chief Inspector for registration in Part B of the general childcare register as a childminder.

(2) An application under subsection (1) must—

(a) give any prescribed information about prescribed matters,

(b) give any other information which the Chief Inspector reasonably requires the applicant to give, and

(c) be accompanied by any prescribed fee.

(3) The Chief Inspector must grant an application under subsection (1) if—

(a) the applicant is not disqualified from registration by regulations under section 75, and

(b) it appears to the Chief Inspector that any requirements prescribed for the purposes of this subsection ("the prescribed requirements for registration") are satisfied and are likely to continue to be satisfied.

(4) The Chief Inspector must refuse any application under subsection (1) which subsection (3) does not require him to grant.

(5) The prescribed requirements for registration may include requirements relating to—

(a) the applicant;

(b) the premises on which the childminding is being (or is to be) provided;

(c) the arrangements for childminding on those premises;

(d) any person who may be caring for children on those premises;

(e) any other person who may be on those premises.

63 Applications for registration on the general register: other childcare providers

(1) A person who provides or proposes to provide on premises in England—

(a) later years provision (other than later years childminding) for a child who has attained the age of eight, or

(b) early years provision or later years provision (other than early years or later years childminding) for a child who has not attained that age but in respect of which the person is not required to be registered under Chapter 2 or 3,

may make an application to the Chief Inspector for registration in Part B of the general childcare register in respect of the premises.

(2) An application under subsection (1) must—

(a) give any prescribed information about prescribed matters;

(b) give any other information which the Chief Inspector reasonably requires the applicant to give;

(c) be accompanied by any prescribed fee.

(3) An application under subsection (1) may not be made in respect of provision for a child who has attained the age of three if—

(a) the provision is made at any of the following schools as part of the school's activities—

(i) a maintained school,

(ii) a school approved by the Secretary of State under section 342 of the Education Act 1996 (c. 56) (approval of non-maintained special schools), or

(iii) an independent school,

(b) the provision is made by the proprietor of the school or a person employed to work at the school, and

(c) the child is a registered pupil at the school or, if the provision is made for more than one child who has attained the age of three, at least one of the children is a registered pupil at the school.

(4) The Chief Inspector must grant an application under subsection (1) if—

(a) the applicant is not disqualified from registration by regulations under section 75, and

(b) it appears to the Chief Inspector that any requirements prescribed for the purposes of this subsection ("the prescribed requirements for registration") are satisfied and are likely to continue to be satisfied.

(5) The Chief Inspector must refuse any application under subsection (1) which subsection (4) does not require him to grant.

(6) The prescribed requirements for registration may include requirements relating to—

(a) the applicant;

(b) the premises on which the childcare is being (or is to be) provided;

(c) the arrangements for childcare on those premises;

(d) any person who may be caring for children on those premises;

(e) any other person who may be on those premises.

64 Entry on the register and certificates

(1) If an application under section 62(1) is granted, the Chief Inspector must—

(a) register the applicant in Part B of the general childcare register as a childminder, and

(b) give the applicant a certificate of registration stating that he is so registered.

(2) If an application under section 63(1) is granted, the Chief Inspector must—

(a) register the applicant in Part B of the general childcare register as a provider of childcare other than a childminder, in respect of the premises in question, and

(b) give the applicant a certificate of registration stating that he is so registered.

(3) A certificate of registration given to the applicant in pursuance of subsection (1) or (2) must contain prescribed information about prescribed matters.

(4) If there is a change of circumstances which requires the amendment of a certificate of registration, the Chief Inspector must give the registered person an amended certificate.

(5) If the Chief Inspector is satisfied that a certificate of registration has been lost or destroyed, the Chief Inspector must give the registered person a copy, on payment by the provider of any prescribed fee.

65 Special procedure for persons already registered

(1) If a person who is registered as a childminder in the early years register or in Part A of the general childcare register gives notice to the Chief Inspector that he wishes to be registered in Part B of the general childcare register, the Chief Inspector must—

(a) register the person in Part B of the general childcare register as a childminder, and

(b) give the applicant a certificate of registration stating that he is so registered.

(2) If a person who is registered (otherwise than as a childminder) in the early years register or in Part A of the general childcare register in respect of particular premises gives notice to the Chief Inspector that he wishes to be registered in Part B of the general childcare register in respect of the same premises, the Chief Inspector must—

(a) register the person in Part B of the general childcare register as a provider of childcare other than a childminder, in respect of the premises, and

(b) give the person a certificate of registration stating that he is so registered.

(3) Subsections (3) to (5) of section 64 apply in relation to a certificate of registration given in pursuance of subsection (1) or (2) of this section as they apply in relation to a certificate of registration given in pursuance of subsection (1) or (2) of that section.

Regulation of persons registering voluntarily

66 Conditions on registration

(1) The Chief Inspector may impose such conditions as he thinks fit on the registration of a person under this Chapter.

(2) The power conferred by subsection (1) may be exercised at the time when the Chief Inspector registers a person in pursuance of section 64 or 65 or at any subsequent time.

(3) The Chief Inspector may at any time vary or remove any condition imposed under subsection (1).

(4) The power conferred by subsection (1) includes power to impose conditions for the purpose of giving effect to regulations under section 67.

(5) A person registered under this Chapter commits an offence if, without reasonable excuse, he fails to comply with any condition imposed under subsection (1).

(6) A person guilty of an offence under subsection (5) is liable on summary conviction to a fine not exceeding level 5 on the standard scale.

67 Regulations governing activities

(1) This section applies to persons providing early years provision or later years provision (or both) in respect of which they are registered under this Chapter.

(2) The Secretary of State may, after consulting the Chief Inspector and any other person he considers appropriate, make regulations governing the activities of persons to whom this section applies.

(3) The regulations may deal with the following matters (among others)—

- (a) the welfare of the children concerned;
- (b) the arrangements for safeguarding the children concerned;
- (c) suitability of persons to care for, or be in regular contact with, the children concerned;
- (d) qualifications and training;
- (e) the suitability of premises and equipment;
- (f) the manner in which the childcare provision is organised;
- (g) procedures for dealing with complaints;
- (h) the keeping of records;
- (i) the provision of information.

(4) The power to make regulations under this section may be exercised so as confer powers or impose duties on the Chief Inspector in the exercise of his functions under this Part.

(5) In particular, it may be so exercised so as to require the Chief Inspector, in exercising his functions under this Part, to have regard to factors, standards and other matters prescribed by or referred to in the regulations.

(6) If the regulations require any person (other than the Chief Inspector) to have regard to or meet factors, standards and other matters prescribed by or referred to in the regulations, they may also provide for any allegation that the person has failed to do so to be taken into account—

- (a) by the Chief Inspector in the exercise of his functions under this Part, or
- (b) in any proceedings under this Part.

CHAPTER 5

COMMON PROVISIONS

Cancellation of registration etc.

68 Cancellation of registration

(1) The Chief Inspector must cancel the registration of a person registered under Chapter 2, 3 or 4 if it appears to him that the person has become disqualified from registration by regulations under section 75.

(2) The Chief Inspector may cancel the registration of a person registered under Chapter 2, 3 or 4 if it appears to him—

(a) that the prescribed requirements for registration which apply in relation to the person's registration under that Chapter have ceased, or will cease, to be satisfied,

(b) that the person has failed to comply with a condition imposed on his registration under that Chapter,

(c) that he has failed to comply with a requirement imposed on him by regulations under that Chapter,

(d) in the case of a person registered under Chapter 2, that he has failed to comply with section 40(2)(a), or

(e) in any case, that he has failed to pay a prescribed fee.

(3) The Chief Inspector may cancel the registration of a person registered as an early years childminder under Chapter 2 if it appears to him that the person has not provided early years childminding for a period of more than three years during which he was registered.

(4) The Chief Inspector may cancel the registration of a person registered as a later years childminder under Chapter 3 if it appears to him that the person has not provided later years childminding for a period of more than three years during which he was registered.

(5) The Chief Inspector may cancel the registration of a person registered as a childminder under Chapter 4 if it appears to him that the person has provided neither early years childminding nor later years childminding for a period of more than three years during which he was registered.

(6) Where a requirement to make any changes or additions to any services, equipment or premises has been imposed on a person registered under Chapter 2, 3 or 4, his registration may not be cancelled on the ground of any defect or insufficiency in the services, equipment or premises if—

(a) the time set for complying with the requirements has not expired, and

(b) it is shown that the defect or insufficiency is due to the changes or additions not having been made.

69 Suspension of registration

(1) Regulations may provide for the registration of a person registered under Chapter 2, 3 or 4 to be suspended for a prescribed period in prescribed circumstances.

(2) Regulations under subsection (1) must include provision conferring on the registered person a right of appeal to the Tribunal against suspension.

(3) A person registered as an early years childminder under Chapter 2 may not provide early years childminding in England at any time when his registration under that Chapter is suspended in accordance with regulations under this section.

(4) A person registered as a later years childminder under Chapter 3 may not provide later years childminding in England, for a child who has not attained the age of eight, at any time when his registration under that Chapter is suspended in accordance with regulations under this section.

(5) Subsection (3) or (4) does not apply in relation to early years childminding or (as the case may be) later years childminding which the person may provide without being registered under Chapter 2 or 3.

(6) A person registered as an early years provider (other than an early years childminder) under Chapter 2 may not provide early years provision on premises in England at any time when his registration under that Chapter in respect of the premises is suspended in accordance with regulations under this section.

(7) A person registered as a later years provider (other than a later years childminder) under Chapter 3 may not provide later years provision on premises in England, for a child who has not attained the age of eight, at any time when his registration under that Chapter in respect of the premises is suspended in accordance with regulations under this section.

(8) Subsection (6) or (7) does not apply in relation to early years provision or (as the case may be) later years provision which the person may provide without being registered under Chapter 2 or 3.

(9) A person commits an offence if, without reasonable excuse, he contravenes subsection (3), (4), (6) or (7).

(10) A person guilty of an offence under subsection (9) is liable on summary conviction to a fine not exceeding level 5 on the standard scale.

(11) In this Part, "the Tribunal" means the Tribunal established by section 9 of the Protection of Children Act 1999 (c. 14).

70 Voluntary removal from register

(1) A person registered under any of Chapters 2 to 4 may give notice to the Chief Inspector that he wishes to be removed from the early years register or (as the case may be) from Part A or B of the general childcare register.

(2) If a person gives notice under subsection (1) the Chief Inspector must remove him from the early years register or (as the case may be) from the relevant Part of the general childcare register.

(3) The Chief Inspector must not act under subsection (2) if—

- (a) the Chief Inspector has sent the person a notice (in pursuance of section 73(2)) of his intention to cancel his registration, and
- (b) the Chief Inspector has not decided that he no longer intends to take that step.

(4) The Chief Inspector must not act under subsection (2) if—

(a) the Chief Inspector has sent the person a notice (in pursuance of section 73(7)) of his decision to cancel his registration, and

(b) the time within which an appeal under section 74 may be brought has not expired or, if such an appeal has been brought, it has not been determined.

(5) Subsections (3) and (4) do not apply if the person is seeking removal from Part B of the general childcare register.

71 Termination of voluntary registration on expiry of prescribed period

Regulations may make provision requiring the Chief Inspector to remove a registered person from Part B of the general childcare register on the expiry of a prescribed period of time from the date of his registration.

Cancellation etc. in an emergency

72 Protection of children in an emergency

(1) In relation to a person registered under Chapter 2, 3 or 4, the Chief Inspector may apply to a justice of the peace for an order—

(a) cancelling the person's registration;

(b) varying or removing a condition to which his registration is subject;

(c) imposing a new condition on his registration.

(2) If it appears to the justice that a child for whom early years provision or later years provision is being or may be provided by that person is suffering or is likely to suffer significant harm, the justice may make the order.

(3) An application under subsection (1) may be made without notice.

(4) An order under subsection (2)—

(a) must be made in writing, and

(b) has effect from the time when it is made.

(5) If an order is made under subsection (2), the Chief Inspector must serve on the registered person as soon as is reasonably practicable after the making of the order—

(a) a copy of the order,

(b) a copy of any written statement in support of the application for the order, and

(c) notice of any right of appeal conferred by section 74.

(6) The documents mentioned in subsection (5) may be served on the registered person by—

(a) delivering them to him, or

(b) sending them by post.

(7) For the purposes of this section, "harm" has the same meaning as in the Children Act 1989 (c. 41) and the question of whether harm is significant is to be determined in accordance with section 31(10) of that Act.

Registration – procedural safeguards

73 Procedure for taking certain steps

(1) This section applies if the Chief Inspector proposes to take any of the following steps under this Part—

(a) refuse an application for registration;

(b) impose a new condition on a person's registration;

(c) vary or remove any condition imposed on a person's registration;

(d) refuse to grant an application for the variation or removal of any such condition;

(e) cancel a person's registration.

(2) The Chief Inspector must give to the applicant or (as the case may be) the registered person notice of his intention to take the step in question.

(3) The notice must—

(a) give the Chief Inspector's reasons for proposing to take the step, and

(b) inform the person concerned of his rights under this section.

(4) The Chief Inspector may not take the step until the end of the period of 14 days beginning with the day on which he gives notice under subsection (2) unless the applicant or (as the case may be) the registered person notifies the Chief Inspector that he does not wish to object to the step being taken.

(5) If the recipient of a notice under subsection (2) ("the recipient") gives notice to the Chief Inspector that he wishes to object to the step being taken, the Chief Inspector must give him an opportunity to object before deciding whether to take the step.

(6) An objection made in pursuance of subsection (5) may be made orally or in writing and in either case may be made by the recipient or his representative.

(7) If the Chief Inspector decides to take the step, he must give the recipient notice of his decision (whether or not the recipient informed the Chief Inspector that he wished to object to the step being taken).

(8) The taking of a step mentioned in paragraph (b), (c) or (e) of subsection (1) does not have effect until—

(a) the expiry of the time within which an appeal may be brought under section 74, or

(b) if such an appeal is brought, the time when the appeal is determined (and the taking of the step is confirmed).

(9) Subsection (8) does not prevent such a step having effect before the expiry of the time within which an appeal may be brought if the person concerned notifies the Chief Inspector that he does not intend to appeal.

(10) If the Chief Inspector gives notice to an applicant for registration under Chapter 2 or 3 that he intends to refuse his application, the application may not be withdrawn without the consent of the Chief Inspector.

(11) In this section and in section 74, "a new condition" means a condition imposed otherwise than at the time of the person's registration.

74 Appeals

(1) An applicant for registration or (as the case may be) a registered person may appeal to the Tribunal against the taking of any of the following steps by the Chief Inspector under this Part—

(a) the refusal of his application for registration;

(b) the imposition of a new condition on his registration;

(c) the variation or removal of any condition imposed on his registration;

(d) the refusal of an application to vary or remove any such condition;

(e) the cancellation of his registration.

(2) An applicant for registration or (as the case may be) a registered person may also appeal to the Tribunal against any other determination made by the Chief Inspector under this Part which is of a prescribed description.

(3) A person against whom an order is made under section 72(2) may appeal to the Tribunal against the making of the order.

(4) On an appeal the Tribunal must either—

(a) confirm the taking of the step, the making of the other determination or the making of the order (as the case may be), or

(b) direct that it shall not have, or shall cease to have, effect.

(5) Unless the Tribunal has confirmed the taking of a step mentioned in subsection (1)(a) or (e) or the making of an order under section 72(2) cancelling a person's registration, the Tribunal may also do either or both of the following—

(a) impose conditions on the registration of the person concerned;

(b) vary or remove any condition previously imposed on his registration.

Disqualification from registration

75 Disqualification from registration

(1) In this section, "registration" means registration under Chapters 2, 3 and 4.

(2) Regulations may provide for a person to be disqualified from registration.

(3) The regulations may, in particular, provide for a person to be disqualified from registration if—

(a) he is included in the list kept under section 1 of the Protection of Children Act 1999 (c. 14);

(b) he is subject to a direction under section 142 of the Education Act 2002 (c. 32) on the grounds that he is unsuitable to work with children or on grounds relating to his health;

(c) an order of a prescribed kind has been made at any time with respect to him;

(d) an order of a prescribed kind has been made at any time with respect to a child who has been in his care;

(e) a requirement of a prescribed kind has been imposed at any time with respect to such a child, under or by virtue of any enactment;

(f) he has at any time been refused registration under Chapter 2, 3 or 4 of this Part of this Act or under Part 10 or Part 10A of the Children Act 1989 (c. 41) or any prescribed enactment, or had any such registration cancelled;

(g) he has been convicted of an offence of a prescribed kind or has been discharged absolutely or conditionally for such an offence;

(h) he has been given a caution in respect of an offence of a prescribed kind;

(i) he has at any time been disqualified from fostering a child privately (within the meaning of the Children Act 1989 (c. 41));

(j) a prohibition has been imposed on him at any time under section 69 of the Children Act 1989, section 10 of the Foster Children (Scotland) Act 1984 (c. 56) or any prescribed enactment;

(k) his rights and powers with respect to a child have at any time been vested in a prescribed authority under a prescribed enactment.

(4) Regulations may provide for a person to be disqualified from registration if—

(a) he lives in the same household as another person who is disqualified from registration, or

(b) he lives in a household in which any such person is employed.

(5) Regulations under subsection (2) or (4) may provide for a person not to be disqualified from registration (and in particular may provide for a person not to be disqualified from registration for the purposes of section 76) by reason of any fact which would otherwise cause him to be disqualified if—

(a) he has disclosed the fact to the Chief Inspector, and

(b) the Chief Inspector has consented in writing to the person's not being disqualified from registration and has not withdrawn his consent.

(6) In this section—

""caution" includes a reprimand or warning within the meaning of section 65 of the Crime and Disorder Act 1998 (c. 37);

"enactment" means any enactment having effect at any time in any part of the United Kingdom.

(7) A conviction in respect of which a probation order was made before 1st October 1992 (which would not otherwise be treated as a conviction) is to be treated as a conviction for the purposes of this section.

76 Consequences of disqualification

(1) This section applies to—

(a) early years provision in respect of which the provider is required by section 33(1) or 34(1) to be registered,

(b) early years provision in respect of which, but for section 34(2), the provider would be required to be registered,

(c) later years provision in respect of which the provider is required by section 52(1) or 53(1) to be registered, and

(d) later years provision in respect of which, but for section 53(2), the provider would be required to be registered.

(2) A person who is disqualified from registration by regulations under section 75 must not—

(a) provide early years or later years provision to which this section applies, or

(b) be directly concerned in the management of early years or later years provision to which this section applies.

(3) No person may employ, in connection with the provision of early years or later years provision to which this section applies, a person who is disqualified from registration by regulations under section 75.

(4) A person who contravenes subsection (2) or (3) commits an offence.

(5) A person who contravenes subsection (2) is not guilty of an offence under subsection (4) if—

(a) he is disqualified from registration by virtue only of regulations under section 75(4), and

(b) he proves that he did not know, and had no reasonable grounds for believing, that he was living—

(i) in the same household as a person who was disqualified from registration, or

(ii) in a household in which such a person was employed.

(6) A person who contravenes subsection (3) is not guilty of an offence under subsection (4) if he proves that he did not know, and had no reasonable grounds for believing, that the person whom he was employing was disqualified from registration.

(7) A person guilty of an offence under subsection (4) is liable on summary conviction to imprisonment for a term not exceeding 51 weeks, or to a fine not exceeding level 5 on the standard scale, or to both.

(8) In relation to an offence committed before the commencement of section 281(5) of the Criminal Justice Act 2003 (c. 44) (alteration of penalties for summary offences), the reference in subsection (7) to 51 weeks is to be read as a reference to 6 months.

Rights of entry

77 Powers of entry

(1) A person authorised for the purposes of this subsection by the Chief Inspector may at any reasonable time enter any premises in England if he has reasonable cause to believe that early years provision or later years provision is being provided on the premises in breach of section 33(1), 34(1), 52(1) or 53(1).

(2) A person authorised for the purposes of this subsection by the Chief Inspector may at any reasonable time enter any premises in England on which early years provision or later years provision in respect of which a person is registered under this Part is being provided—

(a) for the purpose of conducting an inspection under section 49 or 60, or

(b) for the purpose of determining whether any conditions or requirements imposed by or under this Part are being complied with.

(3) Authorisation under subsection (1) or (2)—

(a) may be given for a particular occasion or period;

(b) may be given subject to conditions.

(4) A person entering premises under this section may (subject to any conditions imposed under subsection (3)(b))—

(a) inspect the premises;

(b) inspect, and take copies of—
  (i) any records kept by the person providing the childcare, and
  (ii) any other documents containing information relating to that provision;
(c) seize and remove any document or other material or thing found there which he has reasonable grounds to believe may be evidence of a failure to comply with any condition or requirement imposed by or under this Part;
(d) take measurements and photographs or make recordings;
(e) inspect any children being cared for there, and the arrangements made for their welfare;
(f) interview in private the childcare provider;
(g) interview in private any person caring for children, or living or working, on the premises who consents to be interviewed.

(5) A person entering premises under this section may (subject to any conditions imposed under subsection (3)(b)) require any person to afford him such facilities and assistance with respect to matters within the person's control as are necessary to enable him to exercise his powers under this section.

(6) Section 58 of the Education Act 2005 (c. 18) (inspection of computer records for the purposes of Part 1 of that Act) applies for the purposes of this section as it applies for the purposes of Part 1 of that Act.

(7) A person exercising any power conferred by this section must, if so required, produce a duly authenticated document showing his authority to do so.

(8) A person commits an offence if he intentionally obstructs a person exercising any power under this section.

(9) A person guilty of an offence under subsection (8) is liable on summary conviction to a fine not exceeding level 4 on the standard scale.

(10) In this section, "documents" and "records" each include information recorded in any form.

78 Requirement for consent to entry

(1) This section applies where a person ("the authorised person") proposes to enter domestic premises in pursuance of—
(a) provision made by virtue of section 42(1) and (4) in a learning and development order specifying assessment arrangements in relation to early years provision, or
(b) a power of entry conferred by section 77(2).

(2) If the authorised person has reasonable cause to believe—
(a) that the premises are not the home of the person providing the early years or later years provision, or
(b) that the premises are the home of a child for whom the early years or later years provision is provided,

the authorised person may not enter the premises without the consent of an adult who is an occupier of the premises.

(3) Subsection (2) does not prevent the imposition under section 38, 58 or 66 of a condition requiring a person registered under Chapter 2, 3 or 4 to secure that the occupier of any premises on which the registered person provides early years provision or later years provision gives any consent required by that subsection.

(4) In this section—

"a learning and development order" means an order under section 39(1)(a);

"occupier" does not include the person providing the early years or later years rovision.

79 Power of constable to assist in exercise of powers of entry

(1) A person authorised for the purpose of subsection (1) or (2) of section 77 may apply to a court for a warrant under this section.

(2) If it appears to the court that the authorised person—

(a) has attempted to exercise a power conferred on him by section 77 but has been prevented from doing so, or

(b) is likely to be prevented from exercising any such power,

the court may issue a warrant authorising any constable to assist that person in the exercise of the power, using reasonable force if necessary.

(3) A warrant issued under this section must be addressed to, and executed by, a constable.

(4) Schedule 11 to the Children Act 1989 (c. 41) (jurisdiction of courts) applies in relation to proceedings under this section as if they were proceedings under that Act.

(5) In this section, "court" means the High Court, a county court or a magistrates' court but this is subject to any provision which may be made (by virtue of subsection (4)) by or under Schedule 11 to the Children Act 1989.

Reports and information

80 Combined reports

(1) This section applies if, following inspections under this Part of early years or later years provision, the Chief Inspector—

(a) is required to make more than one report under section 50(1) or determines to make more than one report under section 61(1), or

(b) is required to make one or more reports under section 50(1) and determines to make one or more reports under section 61(1).

(2) If the Chief Inspector considers it appropriate, he may—

(a) combine any two or more of those reports in a single document ("a combined report"), and

(b) to such extent as he considers appropriate, combine the substantive reports.

(3) If the Chief Inspector combines reports under this section, the powers and duties which apply in relation to each report by virtue of section 50(2) or 61(2) are to be read as applying instead to the combined report.

81 Information to be included in annual reports

(1) The annual reports of the Chief Inspector required by section 3(a) of the Education Act 2005 (c. 18) to be made to the Secretary of State must include an account of the exercise of the Chief Inspector's functions under this Part in relation to early years provision and later years provision.

(2) The power conferred on the Chief Inspector by section 3(b) of that Act includes a power to make reports with respect to matters which fall within the scope of his functions by virtue of the provisions of this Part relating to early years provision and later years provision.

82 Supply of information to Chief Inspector

The Chief Inspector may at any time require any person registered under this Part to provide him with any information connected with the person's activities as an early years provider or later years provider which the Chief Inspector considers it necessary to have for the purposes of his functions under this Part.

83 Supply of information to HMRC and local authorities

(1) The Chief Inspector must provide prescribed information to Her Majesty's Revenue and Customs, and the relevant local authority, if he takes any of the following steps under this Part—

(a) grants a person's application for registration;
(b) gives notice of his intention to cancel a person's registration;
(c) cancels a person's registration;
(d) suspends a person's registration;
(e) removes a person from the register at that person's request.

(2) The Chief Inspector must also provide prescribed information to Her Majesty's Revenue and Customs, and the relevant local authority, if an order is made under section 72(2).

(3) The information which may be prescribed for the purposes of this section is—

(a) in the case of information to be provided to Her Majesty's Revenue and Customs, information which Her Majesty's Revenue and Customs may require for the purposes of their functions in relation to tax credits;
(b) in the case of information to be provided to the relevant local authority, information which would assist the local authority in the discharge of their functions under section 12.

(4) In this section, "the relevant local authority" means the English local authority for the area in which the person provides (or, as the case may be, has provided) the early years provision or later years provision in respect of which he is (or was) registered.

84 Disclosure of information for certain purposes

(1) The Chief Inspector may arrange for prescribed information held by him in relation to persons registered under this Part to be made available for the purpose of—41

(a) assisting parents or prospective parents in choosing an early years or later years provider, or

(b) protecting children from harm or neglect.

(2) The information may be made available in such manner and to such persons as the Chief Inspector considers appropriate.

(3) Regulations may require the Chief Inspector to provide prescribed information held by him in relation to persons registered under this Part to prescribed persons for either of the purposes mentioned in subsection (1).

Offences and criminal proceedings

85 Offence of making false or misleading statement

(1) A person commits an offence if, in an application for registration under any of Chapters 2 to 4, he knowingly makes a statement which is false or misleading in a material particular.

(2) A person guilty of an offence under subsection (1) is liable on summary conviction to a fine not exceeding level 5 on the standard scale.

86 Time limit for proceedings

(1) Proceedings for an offence under this Part or regulations made under it may be brought within a period of six months from the date on which evidence sufficient in the opinion of the prosecutor to warrant the proceedings comes to his knowledge.

(2) No such proceedings may be brought by virtue of subsection (1) more than three years after the commission of the offence.

87 Offences by bodies corporate

(1) This section applies where any offence under this Part is committed by a body corporate.

(2) If the offence is proved to have been committed with the consent or connivance of, or to be attributable to any neglect on the part of, any director, manager or other similar officer of the body corporate, or any person who was purporting to act in any such capacity, he (as well as the body corporate) is guilty of the offence and liable to be proceeded against and punished accordingly.

88 Unincorporated associations

(1) Proceedings for an offence under this Part which is alleged to have been committed by an unincorporated association must be brought in the name of the association (and not in the name of any of its members).

(2) For the purpose of any such proceedings, rules of court relating to the service of documents are to have effect as if the association were a body corporate.

(3) In proceedings for an offence under this Part brought against an unincorporated association, section 33 of the Criminal Justice Act 1925 (c. 86) and Schedule 3 to the Magistrates' Courts Act 1980 (c. 43) (procedure) apply as they do in relation to a body corporate.

(4) A fine imposed on an unincorporated association on its conviction of an offence under this Part is to be paid out of the funds of the association.

(5) If an offence under this Part by an unincorporated association is shown—

(a) to have been committed with the consent or connivance of an officer of the association or a member of its governing body, or

(b) to be attributable to any neglect on the part of such an officer or member,

the officer or member as well as the association is guilty of the offence and liable to be proceeded against and punished accordingly.

Miscellaneous

89 Fees

(1) Regulations may require persons registered under any of Chapters 2 to 4 to pay to the Chief Inspector at or by prescribed times fees of the prescribed amounts in respect of the discharge by the Chief Inspector of his functions under this Part.

(2) Regulations under subsection (1) may prescribe circumstances in which—

(a) the amount of a fee payable under the regulations may be varied in accordance with the regulations;

(b) a fee payable under the regulations may be waived.

90 Cases where consent to disclosure withheld

(1) This section applies where the Chief Inspector—

(a) is determining, for the purpose of deciding whether to grant an application for registration under Chapter 2, 3 or 4, whether the prescribed requirements for registration are satisfied and are likely to be continued to be satisfied, or

(b) is determining, for the purpose of deciding whether to cancel the registration of any person under section 68(2)(a), whether the prescribed requirements for registration have ceased, or will cease, to be satisfied.

(2) The Chief Inspector may, if regulations so provide and he thinks it appropriate to do so, treat the prescribed requirements for registration as not being satisfied or (as the case may be) as having ceased to be satisfied if for the purpose of his determination—

(a) the Chief Inspector has requested a person ("A") to consent to the disclosure by another person ("B") to the Chief Inspector of information which—

(i) relates to A,

(ii) is held by B, and

(iii) is of a prescribed description, and

(b) A does not give his consent or withdraws his consent after giving it.

91 Co-operation between authorities

(1) If it appears to the Chief Inspector that any English local authority could, by taking any specified action, help in the exercise of any of his functions under this Part, he may request the help of the authority, specifying the action in question.

(2) An authority whose help is requested must comply with the request if it is compatible with their own statutory and other duties and does not unduly prejudice the discharge of any of their functions.

92 Combined certificates of registration

(1) This section applies if the Chief Inspector is required by virtue of this Part to issue more than one certificate of registration to a person.

(2) If the Chief Inspector considers it appropriate, he may combine any two or more of those certificates in a single certificate (a combined certificate).

(3) A combined certificate of registration must contain prescribed information about prescribed matters.

(4) If there is a change of circumstances which requires the amendment of a combined certificate of registration, the Chief Inspector must give the registered person an amended combined certificate.

(5) If the Chief Inspector is satisfied that a combined certificate of registration has been lost or destroyed, the Chief Inspector must give the registered person a copy, on payment by that person of any prescribed fee.

93 Notices

(1) This section applies in relation to notices required or authorised to be given to any person by any of the following—

- (a) section 57(1) and (2);
- (b) section 65(1) and (2);
- (c) section 70(1);
- (d) section 73(2), (4), (5), (7) and (9).

(2) The notice may be given to the person in question—

- (a) by delivering it to him,
- (b) by sending it by post, or
- (c) subject to subsection (3), by transmitting it electronically.

(3) If the notice is transmitted electronically, it is to be treated as given only if the requirements of subsection (4) or (5) are met.

(4) If the person required or authorised to give the notice is the Chief Inspector—

- (a) the person to whom the notice is required or authorised to be given must have indicated to the Chief Inspector his willingness to receive notices transmitted by electronic means and provided an address suitable for that purpose, and
- (b) the notice must be sent to the address provided by him.

(5) If the person required or authorised to give the notice is not the Chief Inspector, the notice must be transmitted in such manner as the Chief Inspector may require.

(6) An indication given for the purposes of subsection (4) may be given generally for the purposes of notices required or authorised to be given by the Chief Inspector under this Part or may be limited to notices of a particular description.

(7) A requirement imposed by the Chief Inspector under subsection (5) must be published in such manner as the Chief Inspector thinks appropriate for the purpose of bringing it to the attention of persons who are likely to be affected by it.

(8) In relation to the taking of a step mentioned in subsection (1)(b) or (c) of section 73, notification authorised to be given to the Chief Inspector under subsection (4) or (9) of that section may be given orally to a person authorised by the Chief Inspector to receive such notification (as well as by any of the methods mentioned in subsection (2)).

94 Power to amend Part 3: applications in respect of multiple premises

The Secretary of State may by order—

(a) amend this Part so as to enable an application for registration under section 36(1), 55(1) or 63(1) to be made in respect of more than one set of premises, and

(b) make such further amendments of this Part as appear to him to be necessary or expedient in consequence of the amendments made by virtue of paragraph (a).

95 Certain institutions not to be regarded as schools

(1) Section 4 of the Education Act 1996 (c. 56) (schools: general) is amended as follows.

(2) In subsection (1) after "In this Act" insert "(subject to subsection (1A))".

(3) After subsection (1) insert—

"(1A) An institution which—

(a) provides only early years provision (as defined by section 96(2) of the Childcare Act 2006), and

(b) is not a maintained nursery school,

is not a school."

Interpretation

96 Meaning of early years and later years provision etc.

(1) This section applies for the purposes of this Part.

(2) "Early years provision" means the provision of childcare for a young child.

(3) "Early years provider" means a person who provides early years provision.

(4) Subject to subsection (5), "early years childminding" means early years provision on domestic premises for reward (and "early years childminder" is to be read accordingly).

(5) Early years provision on domestic premises for reward is not early years childminding if at any time the number of persons providing the early years provision on the premises or assisting with the provision exceeds three.

(6) "Later years provision", in relation to a child, means the provision of childcare at any time during the period—

(a) beginning with the 1st September next following the date on which he attains the age of five, and

(b) ending with such day as may be prescribed.

(7) "Later years provider" means a person who provides later years provision.

(8) Subject to subsection (9), "later years childminding" means later years provision on domestic premises for reward (and "later years childminder" is to be read accordingly).

(9) Later years provision on domestic premises for reward is not later years childminding if at any time the number of persons providing the later years provision on the premises or assisting with the provision exceeds three.

97 Employees not to be regarded as providing childcare

(1) This section applies for the purposes of this Part.

(2) Where an individual ("the employee") is employed to care for a child by a person who provides early years provision or later years provision for the child, the employee is not to be regarded as providing early years provision or (as the case may be) later years provision by virtue of anything done by him in the course of that employment.

98 Interpretation of Part 3

(1) In this Part—

"the Chief Inspector" means Her Majesty's Chief Inspector of Schools in England;

"childcare" has the meaning given by section 18;

"domestic premises" means premises which are used wholly or mainly as a private dwelling;

"early years provision" has the meaning given by section 96(2);

"early years provider" has the meaning given by section 96(3);

"early years childminding" and "early years childminder" have the meanings given by section 96(4);

"later years provision" has the meaning given by section 96(6);

"later years provider" has the meaning given by section 96(7);

"later years childminding" and "later years childminder" have the meanings given by section 96(8);

"premises" includes any area and any vehicle;

"prescribed" means prescribed by regulations;

"proprietor", in relation to a school, has the same meaning as in the Education Act 1996 (c. 56);

"regulations" means regulations made by the Secretary of State;

"the Tribunal" has the meaning given by section 69(11);

"young child" has the meaning given by section 19.

(2) For the purposes of section 7 of the Interpretation Act 1978 (c. 30) (references to service by post), a notice or order which may by virtue of any provision of this Part be sent by post to an applicant for registration or to a registered person is to be treated as properly addressed if it is addressed to him at the address notified by him to the Chief Inspector as the address to which correspondence to him should be sent.

PART 4

MISCELLANEOUS AND GENERAL

Provision of information about children

99 Provision of information about young children: England

(1) Regulations may make provision, in relation to England, requiring—

(a) a person registered as an early years provider under Chapter 2 of Part 3, and

(b) a person who provides early years provision in respect of which, but for section 34(2) (exemption for provision for children aged 3 or over at certain schools), he would be required to be registered under that Chapter,

to provide to the relevant person such individual child information as may be prescribed.

(2) In subsection (1), "the relevant person" means one or more of the following—

(a) the Secretary of State, and

(b) any prescribed person.

(3) Where any person within paragraph (b) of subsection (2) receives information by virtue of subsection (1), the Secretary of State may require that person to provide any such information—

(a) to the Secretary of State, or

(b) to any prescribed person.

(4) The Secretary of State may provide any individual child information—

(a) to any information collator,

(b) to any prescribed person, or

(c) to any person falling within a prescribed category.

(5) Any information collator—

(a) may provide any individual child information—

(i) to the Secretary of State, or

(ii) to any other information collator, and

(b) may at such times as the Secretary of State may determine or in prescribed circumstances provide such individual child information as may be prescribed—

(i) to any prescribed person, or

(ii) to any person falling within a prescribed category.

(6) Any person holding any individual child information (other than the Secretary of State or an information collator) may provide that information to—

(a) the Secretary of State,

(b) any information collator, or

(c) any prescribed person.

(7) No information received under or by virtue of this section shall be published in any form which includes the name of the child or children to whom it relates.

(8) Regulations under this section may provide that, in such circumstances as may be prescribed, the provision of information to a person other than the Secretary of State is to be treated, for the purposes of any provision of such regulations or this section, as compliance with any requirement imposed by or by virtue of any such provision and relating to the provision of information to the Secretary of State.

(9) In this section—

"early years provision" has the meaning given by section 20;

"individual child information" means information relating to and identifying individual children for whom early years provision is being or has been provided by a person mentioned in subsection (1)(a) or (b), whether obtained under subsection (1) or otherwise;

"information collator" means any body which, for the purposes of or in connection with the functions of the Secretary of State relating to early years provision, is responsible for collating or checking information relating to children for whom such provision is made;

"prescribed" means prescribed by regulations;

"regulations" means regulations made by the Secretary of State.

100 Provision of information about young children: transitory provision

(1) Section 99 has effect with the modifications specified in subsections (2) and (3) until section 7 comes into force.

(2) In subsection (1)—

(a) after "requiring" insert "a person who provides funded nursery education", and

(b) omit paragraphs (a) and (b).

(3) In subsection (9)—

(a) for the definition of "early years provision" substitute—

""funded nursery education" means nursery education, within the meaning of Part 5 of the School Standards and Framework Act 1998 (c. 31), which is provided by any person—

(a) under arrangements made with that person by a local education authority in England in pursuance of the duty imposed on the authority by section 118 of that Act (duty of LEA to secure sufficient nursery education), and

(b) in consideration of financial assistance provided by the authority under those arrangements,

other than such education provided by a school for its pupils;",

(b) for the definition of "individual child information" substitute—

"individual child information" means information relating to and identifying individual children for whom funded nursery education is being or has been provided, whether obtained under subsection (1) or otherwise;", and

(c) in the definition of "information collator" for "early years provision" substitute "funded nursery education".

101 Provision of information about children: Wales

(1) Regulations may make provision, in relation to Wales, requiring—

(a) a person who is registered under Part 10A of the Children Act 1989 (c. 41) to provide child minding or day care, and

(b) a person who provides funded nursery education,

to provide to the relevant person such individual child information as may be prescribed.

(2) In subsection (1), "the relevant person" means one or more of the following—

(a) the Assembly, and

(b) any prescribed person.

(3) Where any person within paragraph (b) of subsection (2) receives information by virtue of subsection (1), the Assembly may require that person to provide any such information—

(a) to the Assembly, or

(b) to any prescribed person.

(4) The Assembly may provide any individual child information—

(a) to any information collator,

(b) to any prescribed person, or

(c) to any person falling within a prescribed category.

(5) Any information collator—

(a) may provide any individual child information—

(i) to the Assembly, or

(ii) to any other information collator, and

(b) may at such times as the Assembly may determine or in prescribed circumstances provide such individual child information as may be prescribed—

(i) to any prescribed person, or

(ii) to any person falling within a prescribed category.

(6) Any person holding any individual child information (other than the Assembly or an information collator) may provide that information to—

(a) the Assembly,

(b) any information collator, or

(c) any prescribed person.

(7) No information received under or by virtue of this section shall be published in any form which includes the name of the child or children to whom it relates.

(8) Regulations under this section may provide that, in such circumstances as may be prescribed, the provision of information to a person other than the Assembly is to be treated, for the purposes of any provision of such regulations or this section, as compliance with any requirement imposed by or by virtue of any such provision and relating to the provision of information to the Assembly.

(9) In this section—

"child minding" and "day care" have the same meaning as in Part 10A of the Children Act 1989;

"funded nursery education" means nursery education, within the meaning of Part 5 of the School Standards and Framework Act 1998 (c. 31), which is provided by any person—

(a) under arrangements made with that person by a local education authority in Wales in pursuance of the duty imposed on the authority by section 118 of that Act (duty of LEA to secure sufficient nursery education), and

(b) in consideration of financial assistance provided by the authority under those arrangements,

other than such education provided by a school for its pupils;

"individual child information" means information relating to and identifying individual children for whom child minding, day care or funded nursery education is being or has been provided, whether obtained under subsection (1) or otherwise;

"information collator" means any body which, for the purposes of or in connection with the functions of the Assembly relating to child minding, day care or funded nursery education (as the case may be), is responsible for collating or checking information relating to children for whom such provision is made;

"prescribed" means prescribed by regulations;

"regulations" means regulations made by the Assembly.

Disqualification for registration under Children Act 1989

102 Disqualification for registration under Children Act 1989

(1) Paragraph 4 of Schedule 9A to the Children Act 1989 (c. 41) (disqualification for registration) is amended as follows.

(2) In sub-paragraph (2)—

(a) in paragraph (b) after "children" insert "or on grounds relating to his health", and

(b) after paragraph (g) insert—

"(ga) he has been given a caution in respect of any offence of a prescribed kind;".

(3) For sub-paragraph (6) substitute—

"(6) In this paragraph—

"caution" includes a reprimand or warning within the meaning of section 65 of the Crime and Disorder Act 1998;

"enactment" means any enactment having effect, at any time, in any part of the United Kingdom."

General

103 Minor and consequential amendments and repeals

(1) Schedule 2 (which contains minor and consequential amendments) has effect.

(2) The enactments specified in Schedule 3 are repealed to the extent specified.

104 Subordinate legislation: general provisions

(1) Any power of the Secretary of State or the Assembly to make an order or regulations under this Act is exercisable by statutory instrument.

(2) Any power of the Secretary of State or the Assembly to make an order or regulations under this Act includes power—

(a) to make different provision for different cases or areas;

(b) to make provision generally or in relation to specific cases;

(c) to make such incidental, supplementary, saving or transitional provision as the Secretary of State or the Assembly thinks fit.

105 Subordinate legislation: parliamentary control

(1) A statutory instrument containing an order or regulations made by the Secretary of State under this Act is subject to annulment in pursuance of a resolution of either House of Parliament.

(2) Subsection (1) does not apply to—

(a) an order under section 109(2) (commencement), or

(b) an order to which subsection (3) applies.

(3) A statutory instrument which contains (whether alone or with other provisions) —

(a) an order under section 5,

(b) an order under section 41(4), or

(c) an order under section 94,

may not be made unless a draft of the instrument has been laid before, and approved by a resolution of, each House of Parliament.

106 General interpretation etc.

In this Act—

"the Assembly" means the National Assembly for Wales;

"child" means a person under the age of 18;

"English local authority" means—

(a) a county council in England;

(b) a metropolitan district council;

(c) a non-metropolitan district council for an area for which there is no county council;

(d) a London borough council;

(e) the Common Council of the City of London (in their capacity as a local authority);

(f) the Council of the Isles of Scilly;

"independent school" has the same meaning as in the Education Act 1996 (c. 56);

"maintained school" means a community, foundation or voluntary school, a community or foundation special school or a maintained nursery school;

"maintained nursery school" has the same meaning as in the School Standards and Framework Act 1998 (c. 31);

"parental responsibility" has the same meaning as in the Children Act 1989 (c. 41);

"registered pupil" has the same meaning as in the Education Act 1996 (c. 56);

"school" has the same meaning as in the Education Act 1996;

"Welsh local authority" means a county council or county borough council in Wales;

"well-being", in relation to children, has the meaning given by section 1(2).

107 Financial provisions

There shall be paid out of money provided by Parliament—

(a) any expenses incurred by a Minister of the Crown or government department under or by virtue of this Act, and

(b) any increase attributable to this Act in the sums which under any other Act are payable out of money so provided.

108 Isles of Scilly

Parts 1 and 3 and this Part, in their application to the Isles of Scilly, have effect subject to such exceptions, adaptations and modifications as the Secretary of State may by order prescribe.

109 Commencement

(1) The following provisions come into force on the day on which this Act is passed—

this section,

sections 104 to 108,

sections 110 and 111, and

paragraph 1 of Schedule 2 (and section 103(1) so far as relating to that paragraph).

(2) The other provisions of this Act come into force in accordance with provision made by order by the appropriate authority (as determined under section 110).

110 The appropriate authority by whom commencement order is made

(1) This section has effect for determining who is the appropriate authority for the purposes of section 109(2).

(2) In relation to Parts 1 and 3 (including Schedule 1) and sections 99 and 100, the appropriate authority is the Secretary of State.

(3) In relation to Part 2 and section 101, the appropriate authority is the Assembly.

(4) In relation to section 102, the appropriate authority is—

(a) in relation to England, the Secretary of State, and

(b) in relation to Wales, the Assembly.

(5) In relation to section 103(1) and Schedule 2, the appropriate authority is—

(a) for paragraphs 18(5)(b) and (c), 20 to 24, 27, 31, 32(4) and 34 of that Schedule (and section 103(1) so far as relating to those provisions)—

(i) in relation to England, the Secretary of State, and

(ii) in relation to Wales, the Assembly,

(b) for paragraph 28 of that Schedule (and section 103(1) so far as relating to that paragraph), the Assembly, and

(c) for the other provisions of that Schedule to which section 109(2) applies (and section 103(1) so far as relating to those provisions), the Secretary of State.

(6) In relation to section 103(2) and Schedule 3, the appropriate authority is—

(a) for a repeal contained in Part 1 of that Schedule, the Secretary of State, and

(b) for a repeal contained in Part 2 of that Schedule, the appropriate authority for the purposes of section 109(2) in relation to the provision on which the repeal is consequential.

111 Short title and extent

(1) This Act may be cited as the Childcare Act 2006.

(2) Any amendment or repeal made by this Act has the same extent as the provision amended or repealed.

(3) Except as provided by subsection (2), this Act extends to England and Wales only.

SCHEDULES

SCHEDULE 1

Section 48

AMENDMENTS RELATING TO THE CURRICULUM

Interpretation

1 In this Schedule "the 2002 Act" means the Education Act 2002 (c. 32).

Education Act 1997 (c. 44)

2 (1) Section 23 of the Education Act 1997 (functions of Qualifications and Curriculum Authority) is amended as follows.

(2) In subsection (1), omit paragraph (c) and the word "and" immediately preceding it.

(3) After subsection (2) insert—

"(2ZA) If the Secretary of State so provides by order, the Qualifications and Curriculum Authority shall also have—

(a) such additional functions as may be specified in the order with respect to pupils falling within subsection (1)(a) or (b) who are young children, and

(b) such functions as may be specified in the order with respect to children not falling within subsection (1)(a) or (b) for whom early years provision is provided in England by early years providers to whom section 40 of the Childcare Act 2006 (duty to implement Early Years Foundation Stage) applies.

(2ZB) Before making an order under subsection (2ZA), the Secretary of State shall consult the Qualifications and Curriculum Authority."

(4) Omit subsection (2A).

(5) In subsection (5)—

(a) for the definition of "funded nursery education" and the "and" immediately following it substitute—

""early years provider" and "early years provision" have the same meaning as in Part 3 of the Childcare Act 2006;", and

(b) at the end insert—

""young children" has the same meaning as in Part 3 of the Childcare Act 2006."

Education Act 2002 (c. 32)

3 (1) Section 76 of the 2002 Act (interpretation of Part 6) is amended as follows.

(2) For the definition of "assessment arrangements" substitute—

""assessment arrangements", in relation to a key stage, means the arrangements for assessing pupils in respect of that stage for the purpose of ascertaining what they have achieved in relation to the attainment targets for that stage;".

(3) Omit the definitions of "early learning goals", "the foundation stage", and "pupil".

(4) In the definition of "school year", omit the words from "and has a corresponding" to the end.

4 Omit section 77 of the 2002 Act (meaning of "nursery education" and related expressions).

5 In section 78 of the 2002 Act (general requirements in relation to the curriculum), omit subsection (2).

6 (1) Section 79 of the 2002 Act (duty to implement general requirements) is amended as follows.

(2) For subsections (1) and (2) substitute—

"(1) The Secretary of State shall exercise his functions with a view to securing that the curriculum for every maintained school or maintained nursery school satisfies the requirements of section 78.

(2) Every local education authority in England shall exercise their functions with a view to securing that the curriculum for every maintained school or maintained nursery school which they maintain satisfies the requirements of section 78."

(3) In subsection (4)(b), omit the words from "or the" to "nursery school".

(4) Omit subsection (5).

7 (1) Section 80 of the 2002 Act (basic curriculum for maintained school) is amended as follows.

(2) In subsection (1)(b), for "who have attained the age of three" substitute "who have ceased to be young children for the purposes of Part 1 of the Childcare Act 2006".

(3) In subsection (2)(a), for "a nursery class in a primary school" substitute "pupils who are under compulsory school age".

8 Omit section 81 of the 2002 Act (the foundation stage).

9 Omit section 83 of the 2002 Act (curriculum requirements for the foundation stage).

10 (1) Section 87 of the 2002 Act (establishment of National Curriculum by order) is amended as follows.

(2) For subsection (1) substitute—

"(1) The Secretary of State shall so exercise the powers conferred by subsection (3) as to revise the National Curriculum for England whenever he considers it necessary or expedient to do so."

(3) Omit subsection (2).

(4) In subsection (4), omit—

(a) "(2) or",

(b) in paragraph (a), the words "the foundation stage or" and "educational programme or", and

(c) in paragraph (b), the words from "(or the timetables" to "education)".

(5) In subsection (5), omit "(2) or".

(6) Omit subsection (6).

(7) In subsection (8), omit "(2)(c) or".

(8) In subsection (10), omit—

(a) "(6) or", and

(b) in paragraph (a) the words from "or" to "provided".

(9) In subsection (11), omit "(2)(c) or" and "(6) or".

11 Omit section 89 of the 2002 Act (implementation in respect of nursery schools etc.).

12 (1) Section 90 of the 2002 Act (development work and experiments) is amended as follows.

(2) In subsection (1), omit "or maintained nursery school".

(3) In subsection (3), omit "or a maintained nursery school".

13 In section 93 of the 2002 Act (temporary exceptions for individual pupils), in subsections (1) and (5), omit "or maintained nursery school".

14 In section 94 of the 2002 Act (information concerning directions under section 93), in subsection (4)(a), omit "or maintained nursery school".

15 In section 96 of the 2002 Act (procedure for making certain orders and regulations), in subsection (1)(a)—

(a) omit "83(3)", and

(b) for "87(2)(a) or (b) or (3)(a) or (b)" substitute "87(3)(a) or (b)".

16 In section 210 of the 2002 Act (orders and regulations)—

(a) omit subsection (3)(c), and

(b) in subsection (5)(b), for "87(2)(c) or (3)(c)" substitute "87(3)(c)".

SCHEDULE 2

Section 103(1)

MINOR AND CONSEQUENTIAL AMENDMENTS

Local Authority Social Services Act 1970 (c. 42)

1 In Schedule 1 to the Local Authority Social Services Act 1970 (social services functions) after the entry relating to the Children Act 1975 insert—

"Adoption Act 1976	Functions continuing to be exercisable by virtue of any transitional or saving

provision made by or under the Adoption and Children Act 2002."

Magistrates' Courts Act 1980 (c. 43)

2 In section 65 of the Magistrates' Courts Act 1980 (meaning of family proceedings), in subsection (1) after paragraph (n) insert—

"(nza) section 72 or section 79 of the Childcare Act 2006;".

Supreme Court Act 1981 (c. 54)

3 In Schedule 1 to the Supreme Court Act 1981 (distribution of business in High Court) in paragraph 3 (which deals with business assigned to the Family Division) after paragraph (e) insert—

"(ea) proceedings under section 79 of the Childcare Act 2006;".

Children Act 1989 (c. 41)

4 In section 18 of the Children Act 1989 (day care for pre-school and other children)—

(a) in subsection (2), after "local authority" insert "in Wales";

(b) in subsection (6), after "local authority" insert "in Wales".

5 In the heading of Part 10A of the Children Act 1989 (child minding and day care for children in England and Wales), omit "England and".

6 In Part 10A of the Children Act 1989 (including Schedule 9A) for "the registration authority", "a registration authority" or "the authority", wherever occurring, substitute (in each case) "the Assembly".

7 In section 79B of the Children Act 1989 (other definitions etc.)—

(a) omit subsection (1),

(b) for subsection (2) substitute—

"(2) In this Act "the Assembly" means the National Assembly for Wales.", and

(c) for subsection (7) substitute—

"(7) "Regulations" means regulations made by the Assembly."

8 In section 79C of the Children Act 1989 (regulations etc. governing child minders and day care providers), omit subsections (1), (4) and (5).

9 In section 79D of the Children Act 1989 (requirement to register)—

(a) for subsection (1) substitute—

"(1) No person shall act as a child minder in Wales unless he is registered under this Part for child minding by the Assembly.",

(b) in subsection (4) omit the words "(whether the contravention occurs in England or Wales)", and

(c) in subsection (5), after "premises" insert "in Wales".

10 In section 79H of the Children Act 1989 (suspension of registration), omit subsection (3).

11 In section 79K of the Children Act 1989 (protection of children in an emergency), in subsection (1) after "registered" insert "under this Part".

12 Omit sections 79N, 79Q and 79R of the Children Act 1989 (which relate only to England).

13 In section 79S of the Children Act 1989 (general functions of the Assembly), in subsection (2) omit the words from "but the regulations" to the end of the subsection.

14 In section 79U of the Children Act 1989 (rights of entry etc.) in subsection (1) omit "England or".

15 In section 79V of the Children Act 1989 (function of local authorities), after "local authority" insert "in Wales".

16 In section 79W of the Children Act 1989 (requirement for certificate of suitability), in subsection (1) after "children" (in the first place where it occurs) insert "in Wales".

17 In section 105 of the Children Act 1989 (interpretation) in subsection (5A)(b) omit "England and".

18 (1) Schedule 9A to the Children Act 1989 (child minding and day care for young children) is amended as follows.

(2) In the heading, after "children" insert "in Wales".

(3) In paragraph 1 (exemption of certain schools), in sub-paragraph (1)(c), omit "the Secretary of State or".

(4) In paragraph 4 (disqualification for registration)—

- (a) in sub-paragraph (1), after "day care" insert "in Wales",
- (b) in sub-paragraph (2)(f), after "Part XA" insert ", or Part 3 of the Childcare Act 2006,",
- (c) in sub-paragraph (3), after "day care" (in each place where it occurs) insert "in Wales",
- (d) in sub-paragraph (4), after "day care" (in each place where it occurs) insert "in Wales", and
- (e) in sub-paragraph (5), after "day care" (in each place where it occurs) insert "in Wales".

(5) In paragraph 5 (offences relating to disqualification)—

- (a) in sub-paragraph (1)(a)—
  - (i) after "child minder" insert "in Wales",
  - (ii) after "child minding" insert "in Wales",
- (b) in sub-paragraph (1)(b) for "any of sub-paragraphs (3) to (5)" substitute "sub-paragraph (4) or (5)", and
- (c) for sub-paragraph (2) substitute—

"(2) A person who contravenes sub-paragraph (4) of paragraph 4 shall not be guilty of an offence under this paragraph if—

- (a) he is disqualified for registration by virtue only of regulations made under sub-paragraph (3) of paragraph 4, and
- (b) he proves that he did not know, and had no reasonable grounds for believing, that he was living in the same household as a person who was disqualified for

registration or in a household in which such a person was employed."

(6) In paragraph 6 (certificates of registration), in sub-paragraph (5)—

(a) in paragraph (a) for "(in England or in Wales)" substitute "in Wales", and

(b) in paragraph (b) after "any premises" insert "in Wales".

(7) In paragraph 8 (co-operation between authorities), omit sub-paragraph (1).

Water Industry Act 1991 (c. 56)

19 In Schedule 4A to the Water Industry Act 1991 (premises that are not to be disconnected for non-payment of charges) for paragraph 12 substitute—

"12 (1) Premises in England which are used for the provision of childcare by a person who is registered (otherwise than as a childminder) under Part 3 of the Childcare Act 2006 in respect of the premises.

(2) Premises in Wales which are used for the provision of day care for children by a person who is registered under Part 10A of the Children Act 1989 in respect of the premises."

Education Act 1996 (c. 56)

20 In the heading to section 17 of the Education Act 1996, for "nursery education" substitute "nursery schools".

21 In section 318 of the Education Act 1996 (provision of goods and services in connection with special educational needs), in subsection (3A)(a) for "receiving relevant nursery education" substitute "receiving relevant early years education".

22 (1) Section 329A of the Education Act 1996 (review or assessment of educational needs at request of responsible body) is amended as follows.

(2) In subsection (11), for "relevant nursery education" substitute "relevant early years education".

(3) In subsection (13)(c), for "nursery", in both places, substitute "early years".

(4) For subsection (14) substitute—

"(14) "Relevant early years education"—

(a) in relation to England, has the same meaning as it has (in relation to England) in section 123 of the School Standards and Framework Act 1998 except that it does not include early years education provided by a local education authority at a maintained nursery school for a pupil at the school;

(b) in relation to Wales, has the same meaning as it has (in relation to Wales) in section 123 of the School Standards and Framework Act 1998 except that it does not include early years education provided by a local education authority at a maintained nursery school."

23 In section 509A of the Education Act 1996 (travel arrangements for children receiving nursery education otherwise than at school)—

(a) in the heading and in each of subsections (1), (3) and (4) for "nursery education" substitute "early years education", and

(b) for subsection (5) substitute—

"(5) In this section "relevant early years education" means—

(a) in relation to England, early years provision as defined by section 20 of the Childcare Act 2006 which is provided under arrangements made by a local authority in England in pursuance of the duty imposed by section 7 of that Act (whether or not the local authority provides the early years provision);

(b) in relation to Wales, nursery education which is provided—

(i) by a local education authority in Wales, or

(ii) by any other person who is in receipt of financial assistance given by a local authority under arrangements made by them in pursuance of the duty imposed by section 118 of the School Standards and Framework Act 1998."

24 In section 512 of the Education Act 1996 (LEA functions concerning provision of meals etc.)—

(a) in subsection (1)(c) for "relevant funded nursery education" substitute "relevant funded early years education", and

(b) in subsection (6) for the definition of "relevant funded nursery education" substitute—

""relevant funded early years education", in relation to a local education authority in England, means early years provision as defined by section 20 of the Childcare Act 2006 which is provided by a person, other than the governing body of a maintained school (within the meaning of section 20(7) of the School Standards and Framework Act 1998) or a maintained nursery school, under arrangements made by a local authority in pursuance of the duty imposed by section 7 of the 2006 Act (duty to secure prescribed early years provision free of charge);

"relevant funded early years education", in relation to a local education authority in Wales, means education provided by a person other than the governing body of a maintained school (within the meaning of section 20(7) of the School Standards and Framework Act 1998) or a maintained nursery school—

(a) under arrangements made with that person by the authority in pursuance of the duty imposed on the authority by section 118 of that Act (duty of LEA to secure sufficient nursery education), and

(b) in consideration of financial assistance provided by the authority under those arrangements."

25 (1) Section 515 of the Education Act 1996 (provision of teaching services for day nurseries) is amended as follows.

(2) In subsection (1) after "a day nursery" insert "in England or Wales or to a registered early years provider in England".

(3) In subsection (3)—

(a) in paragraph (b) after "the day nursery" insert "or (as the case may be) the registered early years provider", and

(b) in paragraph (c) for the words from "including" to the end of the paragraph substitute "including—

(i) in relation to England, any charges to be imposed in connection with the arrangements, and

(ii) in relation to Wales, where the teacher's school and the day nursery are in the areas of different local education authorities, financial adjustments between those authorities."

(4) For subsection (4) substitute—

"(4) In this section—

"day nursery" means a day nursery provided under section 18 of the Children Act 1989 (provision by local authorities of day care for pre-school and other children);

"registered early years provider" means a person registered under Part 3 of the Childcare Act 2006."

26 (1) Section 535 of the Education Act 1996 (provision of teaching services for day nurseries) is amended as follows.

(2) In subsection (1) after "a day nursery" insert "in England or Wales or to a registered early years provider in England".

(3) In subsection (3)—

(a) in paragraph (b) after "the day nursery" insert "or (as the case may be) the registered early years provider", and

(b) in paragraph (c) for the words from "including" to the end of the paragraph substitute "including—

(i) in relation to England, any charges to be imposed in connection with the arrangements, and

(ii) in relation to Wales, where the teacher's school and the day nursery are in the areas of different local education authorities, financial adjustments between those authorities."

(4) For subsection (4) substitute—

"(4) In this section—

"day nursery" means a day nursery provided under section 18 of the Children Act 1989 (provision by local authorities of day care for pre-school and other children);

"registered early years provider" means a person registered under Part 3 of the Childcare Act 2006."

27 (1) Section 548 of the Education Act 1996 (no right to give corporal punishment) is amended as follows.

(2) In subsection (1)(c) for "specified nursery education" substitute "specified early years education".

(3) For subsection (8) substitute—

"(8) "Specified early years education" means—

(a) in relation to England, early years provision as defined by section 20 of the Childcare Act 2006 which is provided under arrangements made by a local authority in England in pursuance of the duty imposed by section 7 of that Act (whether or not the local authority provides the early years provision);

(b) in relation to Wales, full-time or part-time education suitable for children who have not attained compulsory school age which is provided—

(i) by a local education authority in Wales, or

(ii) by any other person who is in receipt of financial assistance given by such an authority under arrangements made by them in pursuance of the duty imposed by section 118 of the School Standards and Framework Act 1998."

Education Act 1997 (c. 44)

28 In section 38 of the Education Act 1997 (inspection of local education authorities), in subsection (2A)(b), after "sections 25 and 26" insert "of the Children Act 2004".

Police Act 1997 (c. 50)

29 In section 113F of the Police Act 1997 (criminal record certificates: supplementary), in subsection (1)—

(a) before paragraph (a) insert—

"(za) for the purposes of Part 3 of the Childcare Act 2006 (regulation of provision of childcare in England) and regulations made under it, the applicant's suitability to look after or be in regular contact with children;",

(b) in paragraph (a), omit the words "England and", and

(c) in paragraph (c) omit the words "section 71 of the Children Act 1989 or".

School Standards and Framework Act 1998 (c. 31)

30 In section 118 of the School Standards and Framework Act 1998 (duty of LEA as respects availability of nursery education)—

(a) in subsection (1) after "a local education authority" insert "in Wales", and

(b) in subsection (2)(b) for "the Secretary of State" substitute "the National Assembly for Wales".

31 Section 118A of the School Standards and Framework Act 1998 (duties of LEA in respect of childcare) is omitted.

32 (1) Section 119 of the School Standards and Framework Act 1998 (early years development and childcare partnerships) is amended as follows.

(2) In subsection (1), after "local education authority" insert "in Wales".

(3) In subsection (2), for "the Secretary of State" substitute "the Assembly".

(4) In subsection (5), omit paragraph (ab).

(5) In subsection (6), for "The Secretary of State" substitute "The Assembly".

33 (1) Section 122 of the School Standards and Framework Act 1998 (inspection of nursery education) is amended as follows.

(2) In the heading, after "nursery education" insert "in Wales".

(3) In subsection (1), after "nursery education" insert "in Wales".

34 In section 123 of the School Standards and Framework Act 1998 (children with special educational needs)—

(a) in subsections (1)(a), (2) and (3A) for "relevant nursery education" substitute "relevant early years education", and

(b) for subsection (4) substitute—

"(4) In this section "relevant early years education" means—

(a) in relation to England, early years provision as defined by section 20 of the Childcare Act 2006 which is provided under arrangements made by a local authority in England in pursuance of the duty imposed by section 7 of that Act (whether or not the local authority provides the early years provision);

(b) in relation to Wales, nursery education which is provided—

(i) by a local education authority in Wales, or

(ii) by any other person who is in receipt of financial assistance given by such an authority under arrangements made by them in pursuance of the duty imposed by section 118."

35 In section 142 of the School Standards and Framework Act 1998 (general interpretation) for subsection (5) substitute—

"(5) For the purposes of this Act children are to be regarded as admitted to a school for nursery education if—

(a) in the case of a school in England, they are admitted for early years provision as defined by section 20 of the Childcare Act 2006 and are not, or are not to be, placed on admission in a reception class or any more senior class, and

(b) in the case of a school in Wales, if they are, or are to be, placed on admission in a nursery class."

36 (1) Schedule 26 to the School Standards and Framework Act 1998 (inspection of nursery education) is amended as follows.

(2) In the title of the Schedule after "nursery education" insert "in Wales".

(3) In paragraph 1(1)—

(a) in paragraph (za) after "school" (in each place where it occurs) insert "in Wales";

(b) in paragraph (a) after "local education authority" insert "in Wales";

(c) in paragraph (b) after "local education authority" insert "in Wales".

(4) In paragraph 1(2) after "local education authority" insert "in Wales".

(5) In paragraph 1(3)(b)(ii) after "local education authority" insert "in Wales".

(6) In paragraph 2(1)—

(a) omit paragraph (a), and

(b) for paragraph (c) substitute—

"(c) "the Chief Inspector" (without more) means the Chief Inspector for Wales."

(7) For paragraph 2(5) substitute—

"(5) In this Schedule, "well-being" in relation to children for whom nursery education is provided in Wales, is a reference to their well-being having regard to the matters mentioned in section 25(2) of the Children Act 2004."

(8) In paragraph 3 for "the Secretary of State" substitute "the Assembly".

(9) In paragraph 4—

(a) for "the Secretary of State" (in both places where it occurs) substitute "the Assembly", and

(b) for "the Secretary of State's" substitute "the Assembly's".

(10) In paragraph 5 for "the Secretary of State" substitute "the Assembly".

(11) Omit the following—

(a) paragraph 6A,

(b) in the cross-heading before paragraph 7, the words "6A or",

(c) in paragraph 7, the words "6A or",

(d) paragraph 13A,

(e) paragraph 14(1),

(f) in paragraph 16, the words "6A or", and

(g) in paragraph 18, sub-paragraphs (1)(a) and (4)(a).

Protection of Children Act 1999 (c. 14)

37 In section 2A of the Protection of Children Act 1999 (power of certain authorities to refer individuals for inclusion in list of persons considered unsuitable to work with children), in subsection (1)(a) for "or Part XA of the Children Act 1989" substitute ", Part 10A of the Children Act 1989 or Part 3 of the Childcare Act 2006".

38 In section 9 of the Protection of Children Act 1999 (the Tribunal), in subsection (2)—

(a) omit the "or" at the end of paragraph (e), and

(b) at the end of paragraph (f) insert "or

(g) on an appeal under, or by virtue of, Part 3 of the Childcare Act 2006."

Criminal Justice and Court Services Act 2000 (c. 43)

39 In section 36 of the Criminal Justice and Court Services Act 2000 (meaning of "regulated position") in subsection (13) for paragraph (c) substitute—

"(c) in relation to England—

(i) a person registered under Part 3 of the Childcare Act 2006, otherwise than as a childminder, for providing care on premises on which the child is cared for,

(ii) a person registered under Part 3 of that Act as a childminder who is providing early years or later years childminding (within the meaning of that Part of that Act) for the child,

(ca) in relation to Wales, a person registered under Part 10A of the Children Act 1989 for providing day care on premises on which the child is cared for, and".

40 In section 42 of the Criminal Justice and Court Services Act 2000 (interpretation of Part 2) in subsection (1) for the definition of "day care premises" substitute—

""day care premises" means—

(a) in relation to England, premises in respect of which a person is registered, otherwise than as a childminder, under Part 3 of the Childcare Act 2006,

(b) in relation to Wales, premises in respect of which a person is registered under Part 10A of the Children Act 1989 for providing day care,".

Education Act 2002 (c. 32)

41 In section 153 of the Education Act 2002 (powers of LEA in respect of funded nursery education)—

(a) in subsection (1), after "local education authority" insert "in Wales", and

(b) in subsection (2)(a), omit "the Secretary of State or (as respects local education authorities in Wales)".

42 In section 176 of the Education Act 2002 (consultation with pupils) in subsection (3) for the definition of "pupil" substitute—

""pupil" does not include a child who is being provided with early years education (whether at a school or elsewhere) and, for this purpose, "early years education" means—

(a) in relation to England, early years provision as defined by section 20 of the Childcare Act 2006, and

(b) in relation to Wales, nursery education."

Children Act 2004 (c. 31)

43 In section 12 of the Children Act 2004 (information databases) in subsection (8) for paragraph (a) substitute—

"(a) a person registered under Part 3 of the Childcare Act 2006 (regulation of provision of childcare in England);".

Education Act 2005 (c. 18)

44 In section 59(1) of the Education Act 2005 (combined reports)—

(a) in paragraph (b) after "for children" insert "in Wales",

(b) in paragraph (c) after "nursery education" insert "in Wales",

(c) omit the "and" at the end of paragraph (c), and

(d) at the end of paragraph (d) insert "and

(e) Chapters 2 and 3 of Part 3 of the Childcare Act 2006 (regulation of early years and later years provision in England)."

SCHEDULE 3

Section 103(2)

REPEALS

PART 1

THE CURRICULUM

Short title and chapter	*Extent of repeal*
Education Act 1997 (c. 44)	In section 23— in subsection (1), paragraph (c) and the word "and" immediately preceding it; and subsection (2A).
Education Act 2002 (c. 32)	In section 76, the definitions of "early learning goals", "the foundation stage", and "pupil" and, in the definition of "school year", the words from "and has a corresponding" to the end.
	Section 77.
	Section 78(2).
	In section 79— in subsection (4)(b), the words from "or the" to "nursery school"; and subsection (5).
	Section 81.
	Section 83.
	In section 87— subsection (2); in subsection (4), the words "(2) or", in paragraph (a) the words "the foundation stage or" and "educational programme or" and in paragraph (b) the words from "(or the timetables" to "education)"; in subsection (5), the words "(2) or"; subsection (6); in subsection (8), the words "(2)(c) or"; in subsection (10), the words "(6) or" and, in paragraph (a), the words from "or" to "provided"; and

Short title and chapter	Extent of repeal
	in subsection (11), the words "(2)(c) or" and "(6) or".
	Section 89.
	In section 90, in subsection (1) the words "or maintained nursery school" and in subsection (3) the words "or a maintained nursery school".
	In section 93(1) and (5), the words "or maintained nursery school".
	In section 94(4)(a), the words "or maintained nursery school".
	In section 96(1)(a), the words "83(3),".
	Section 210(3)(c).
	In Schedule 17, paragraph 1(4) to (6).

PART 2

OTHER REPEALS

Short title and chapter	Extent of repeal
Children Act 1989 (c. 41)	In the heading of Part 10A, the words "England and".
	Section 79B(1).
	Section 79C(1), (4) and (5).
	In section 79D(4), the words "(whether the contravention occurs in England or Wales)".
	Section 79H(3).
	Section 79N.
	Sections 79Q and 79R.
	In section 79S(2), the words from "but the regulations" to the end of the subsection.
	In section 79U(1), the words "England or".
	In section 105(5A)(b) the words "England and".
	In Schedule 9A— (a) in paragraph 1(1)(c), the words "the Secretary of State or", and (b) paragraph 8(1).
Police Act 1997 (c. 50)	In section 113F(1)—

Short title and chapter	*Extent of repeal*
	(a) in paragraph (a), the words "England and", and (b) in paragraph (c), the words "section 71 of the Children Act 1989 or".
School Standards and Framework Act 1998 (c. 31)	Section 118A.
	Section 119(5)(ab).
	In Schedule 26— (a) paragraph 2(1)(a); (b) paragraph 6A; (c) in the cross-heading before paragraph 7, the words "6A, or"; (d) in paragraph 7, the words "6A or"; (e) paragraph 13A; (f) paragraph 14(1); (g) in paragraph 16, the words "6A or"; (h) in paragraph 18, sub-paragraphs (1)(a) and (4)(a).
Protection of Children Act 1999 (c. 14)	In section 9(2), the word "or" at the end of paragraph (e).
Education Act 2002 (c. 32)	Section 149(1).
	Section 150(1).
	In section 153(2)(a) the words "the Secretary of State or (as respects local education authorities in Wales)".
Children Act 2004 (c. 31)	In section 18(2), the word "and" at the end of paragraph (d).
	In section 23(3), the word "and" at the end of paragraph (b).
Education Act 2005 (c. 18)	In section 59(1), the word "and" at the end of paragraph (c).
	In Schedule 7, paragraphs 1, 3, 4 and 10(6).

Adapted and published by GRANGIS under the OGL Licence 3.0.

www.nationalarchives.gov.uk/doc/open-government-licence/version/3/

GRANGIS - UK PUBLISHING 2022.
Thank you for taking the time to leave us a review regarding this version

★★★★★

For further inquiries, contact us at:
www.grangis.com / contact@grangis.com

www.ingramcontent.com/pod-product-compliance
Lightning Source LLC
LaVergne TN
LVHW060213210926
848481LV00008B/2730
* 9 7 9 8 8 8 5 5 9 0 7 6 1 *